MORE MEDIEVAL BYWAYS

MORE
MEDIEVAL BYWAYS

BY

L. F. SALZMAN, F.S.A.

METHUEN & CO. LTD.
36 ESSEX STREET W.C.
LONDON

First Published in 1926

PRINTED IN GREAT BRITAIN

GEORGIO KRUGER GRAY

ILLUSTRANDO ILLUSTRI,
JOCANDO JUCUNDO,
AMICO AMATO,
HUNC LIBRUM
DEDICO.

Author's Note ✧ ✧ ✧ ✧ ✧

IN 1913 I published a little volume of half a dozen essays, under the title, "Medieval Byways," dealing lightly with the more fantastic side of life in the Middle Ages. The kindness, even enthusiasm, with which the book was received by the critics encouraged me to continue, rather desultorily, to write in the same strain. The essays here collected appeared in the extinct *British Review* and in *Blackwood's* and *The Cornhill*, to whose proprietors I am indebted for permission to republish them. Like their predecessors, they are woven round passages and phrases in original records or ancient books, whose quaintness or humanity caught my wandering fancy; like them, also, their purpose is to amuse and interest, and possibly to help their readers to enjoy the fascination of the Middle Ages.

L. F. S.

Cambridge, August 1926

Contents ✦ ✦ ✦ ✦ ✦ ✦

MORE
MEDIEVAL BYWAYS

I.   Sidelights on History   ᴓ   ᴓ   ᴓ

HISTORY, as taught a generation since, meant battles and the doings of kings.   Then arose a new school of historians who spelt the People with a big P, and declared that the real History was concerned with merchants and citizens and lawyers and peasants, but not at all with the chance occupants of thrones and their struggles to dispossess one another.   So they wrote learnedly of ships and shoes and sealing-wax and also of cabbages, but hardly at all, or at best but incidentally, of kings.   Now there are as many ways of writing History as of constructing tribal lays, but it is notorious that they are not all right. Hitherto, however, no man has decided with authority which ways are right and which wrong. nor is there any prospect that any will ever do so. But if the opinions of those who read history were to be taken it is probable that we should find a distinct preference expressed for those works in which the personal touch is most prominent. Philosophers may be interested in facts, which serve as building materials for their own theories or as half-bricks for battering their opponents, and schoolboys in acts, but the general reader has an undoubted liking for persons.   One result of

I

this is the enormous output at the present time of
biographies and monographs on worthy, or prefer-
ably unworthy, men and women. Of course this
is in part due to the present being an age of
specialisation, so that whereas Raleigh was content
calmly to undertake a History of the World in
the enforced seclusion of the Tower, the present-
day writer ransacks the archives of a dozen
countries to compile a " contribution towards the
history " of some obscure damsel who once took
a too amorous king's fancy. But apart from this
rage for microscopic detail, which is a modern
disease, there is the longing for those little intimate
touches which make the figures of history seem
human and real. The old chroniclers felt this,
and from classic times downwards have not failed
to give the exact words of their heroes on critical
occasions, even when it was clearly impossible for
them to have known them. To this same feeling
we owe the cakes of Alfred, the ride of Godiva and
the pleasing but entirely fabulous story of the
Saracen mother of St. Thomas Becket arriving
in this country with no knowledge of English
beyond her husband's telegraphic address,
" Gilbert, London." Nor let anyone imagine
that I wish to imply that this attitude on the part
of the general reader is to be reprobated. On
the contrary, I share it, and it gives me much
pleasure to find, for instance, that Henry III had
a greater appreciation of fresh air than the average
German, and insisted on having the glass windows
opposite his bed at Winchester made so as to open.
The Black Prince is so identified with martial
exploits that it is almost a relief to find that he
once had a nursery in the palace of Guildford, like

any other child, and our belief in that bibulous old
ruffian Falstaff with his intolerable quantity of sack
to a pennyworth of bread must be strengthened
by finding that in the household accounts of his
boon companion, Prince Hal, thirteen shillings-
worth of bread is set off by seventy pounds-worth
of romney, bastard and malvoisie and wine of
Gascony, with an additional nineteen hundred
gallons of ale, doubtless for the refreshment of
Nym, Bardolf and their fellows.

There is another kind of personalities which
appeals to me more than these sidelights on
persons of importance. When we have a record
of how some of the outstanding events of medieval
times affected obscure individuals we get into
touch with that elusive and interesting personage,
the man in the street. What one really wants
to know about any historic event is how it struck
contemporaries, and although it may be true that
" whosoever in writing a modern history shall
follow Truth too near the heels it may haply strike
out his teeth," and that therefore the contemporary
chronicler will most likely colour his narrative with
a wise consideration for the feelings of the party
in power, yet he will the more for that be free from
the vice of impartiality, which is alike misleading
and emasculating. Contemporary chronicles are
therefore valuable although they are written with
one eye on the public and one on the powers that
be ; but still more enlightening are casual references
in records and legal documents. Full as these are
of prejudice and inaccuracy, the events which for
us are historic are in them mere incidents of common knowledge, only important in their indirect
effects. The wars of the three Henries with

More Medieval Byways

France, for instance, affected Walter Orpyngton because, having been taken prisoner several times, he lost much goods and " felle in grete age and povertee and litell hath wherewith hym to helpe and susteyne," after serving continually in France and Normandy for thirty-six years, including the siege of Harfleur. From which siege, Henry V with " hys lyttylle blessyd mayne " marched to the field of Agincourt. At that famous but futile victory, when the English, for the loss of a duke, an earl, two knights and Davy Gam, slew or captured the greater part of the French noblesse, John Craven and Simon Irby secured certain prisoners of value. They were therefore justifiably annoyed when William Bukton, esquire, forcibly carried off their prisoners and set them to ransom, and were no doubt pleased to be able to point out that Bukton had not paid to the crown his share from the ransom, which ought apparently to have been returned under " Schedule D," or its medieval equivalent. In view of the amount of pillage gained by the English at this battle it is interesting to notice that King Henry's sergeant of the pantry, John Haregrove, lost in the confusion a salt-cellar of gold of " morask " work garnished with amethysts, garnets, rubies and emeralds, which had been given by the Bishop of Norwich ; also an enamelled gold salt weighing nearly three pounds, three gilt salts enamelled with the fourth Henry's badge of the swan, and a number of spoons.

If Agincourt had no other result, and probably no other victory so sweepingly complete ever achieved such shortlived effects, it at least demonstrated the importance of infantry. The battle was won by the humble foot soldiers at the expense of the mounted nobility. The lesson must have been a bitter one for the gentry, whose arm the cavalry has been ever since the Norman knights of William overthrew Harold and his earth-treading Saxons at Hastings, and they certainly would not have concurred with Lord Mayor Gregory that "as for spereman they ben good to ryde before the footemen and ete and drynke uppe hyr vetayle, and many moo suche prety thyngys they doo, hold me excusyd thoughe I say the beste, for in the fote men ys alle the tryste." Too often it was the fate of the foot soldier to bear the brunt of many battles, and then to be treated like Walter Orpyngton, already alluded to, or like the garrison of Brest. When Richard II gave up that town in 1396 the garrison returned to London, and finding that the King was holding " a sumptuous feest " in Westminster Hall some of them determined to have at least one good meal, and pressing into the Hall seized a table. Then the Duke of Gloucester said to his royal nephew, " Syr, have ye not seen the felowes that satte in so great noumbre to-day in your halle at such a table ? " When the King " axyd of the Duke what company it was," he replied, " Syr, these ben your sowdyours comyn from Brest and as nowe have nothynge to take to, nor knowe not howe to shyft for theyr lyvyng, and the rather for that, as I am enfourmyd, they have ben before tyme evyll payed." Half a century later the " poor souldeours " of Caen complained that for ten months they had received no pay, although the three estates of the Duchy of Normandy, in order that they might be " unrobbed and unpilled," had voted the money for the " garneson " as well as for Lord Hastings and his fellow commissioners. Hastings took care of himself and left the garrison unpaid, so that to fill their empty purses they were " fayn to aventur theym upon the Kynges enemyes, that some were taken prysoner, some mordered and slayn, some sworn Frenssh, for defaute of payment. And thoo that hadde no horse ne harnys robbed and pilled the Kinges true subjects," which the complainants considered, with much justice, was one of the causes of the loss of the Duchy. An unpaid soldiery living by pillage soon alienate the populace exposed to their raids. Even the inevitable hardships of a siege will shake the allegiance of men who never having got any good from those to whom, as they are informed, the ties of patriotism should bind them, have little to lose by a change of masters and much to fear from a lengthened resistance. When Henry V besieged Rouen.

> Hyr brede was fulle ny gone,
> And flesche save hors had they non.
> They etete doggys, they ete cattys,
> They ete mysse, horse and rattys.
> For 3od. went a ratte,
> For 2 noblys went a catte,
> For 6d. went a mouse ;
> They left but fewe in any house.
> A negge at 9d., a nappylle at 10,
> Such a market was amonge thes men.

It was no wonder, therefore, that when King Henry, to celebrate Christmas Day, provided ample supplies of food outside the walls and invited all the poor of the city to come and feed that

" Amyghty God," they saydyn then,
" Of tender hertys ben Englysche men.
" Lo, here oure excellent Kynge
" That we have ben so long stondynge,
" Of us nowe hathe more compassyon
" Thenn hathe oure owne nacyon.
" That God as thou art fulle of myght,
" Graunt hym grace to wynne hys ryght."

Not only did they express pious hopes for his victory, but when their leaders broke off negotiations for surrender

The poore people alle aboute
On the ryche made a schoute,
" But ye acorde wyth youre wylle,
" He shall come in thoughe ye nylle.
" Your styffegates that ye steke,
" We shalle them burn and up breke.
" We shall lat hym in to hys ryght ;
" If ye defende we shall fyght,
" Levyr than thys to byde here,
" And dy for hunger alle in fere."

And so " Monsenoure Gy the Botlere " was enforced to yield up the city of Rouen, and Normandy was once more united to England under Henry V, only to be lost beyond recall by his feeble son and his untrustworthy ministers, the culminating blow being the disaster of Fourmigny, where that " manly knyght," Sir Thomas Kyriel, was captured with " alle the legge harneyse." It was " at the tyme of the distrussynge of Sir Thomas Keryell " that John Swan of Sewsterne in Lincolnshire was taken prisoner and cast into dure prison at " Caryngton," which I suppose is English for

Charenton. There he was set to ransom at " 50 scutes, a mark of silver and 6 bonettys of scarlet " —Lincoln being famous for its scarlet from the twelfth century—and was also made surety for 26 " salutes " due for the ransom of John Hayward, who had gone to England and not returned to pay his ransom. So John's good neighbour, Thomas Sewsterne, sought licence to gather alms for the raising of these sums, which must be paid by Whitsun or else John Swan " must nedys be sworne Frenshe or utterly dye."

It was the disastrous defeat of Fourmigny which drove the exasperated nation to demand the impeachment of Suffolk and led to his execution by the Kentish shipmen ; and it was fear of the consequences of this act, combined with other good reasons, that led to the rising of the commons under Jack Cade. The failure of that rising was largely due, as in the case of the earlier Peasants' Rebellion and the later Pilgrimage of Grace, to the fact that the moving spirits were loyal to the King and only anxious to attack his ministers, and were therefore in the impossible position of conservative revolutionaries. In their declaration they set forth that " they call us risers and treyturs and the Kynge's enemys, but we schalbe founde his trew lege mene and his best freendis with the help of Jesu, to Whome we crye dayly and nygtly, with mony thousand moe, that God of hys rygtwysnesse schall take vengeaunse on the false treyturs of his ryalle realme that have brougt us in this myschief and myserie." Yet even in this declaration, for all its careful profession of loyalty, there is a pretty clear indication that there was no particular respect for his intellect and that he was regarded as a helpless tool in the hands of his advisers. "By the satiables covetises melicious pompuses in false and noughte broughte up dayly and nyghtely aboute his hyghnesse, the same dayly and nygthly is enformed that good is evulle and evulle good." Moreover "our soveraygne lorde may wele undurstand that he hath hadde false counsayle, for his lordez ern lost, his marchundize is lost, his comyns destroyed, the see is lost, Fraunse is lost, himself so pore that he may not for his mete nor drynk; he oweth more than evur dyd Kynge in Inglond and yit dayly his traytours that beene aboute hym waytethe wherever thynge schudde coome to hyme by his lawe and they aske it from hyme." The opinion thus hinted at was put more bluntly by William Merfeld in Brightling market, when he said that the king "was a naterell foole and wolde ofte tymes holde a staff in his handes with a bird on the ende, playing therewith as a foole." So also Harry Mase, a German weaver of Ely, declared that the king "lokyd more lyke a childe than a man," and that he "within shorte tyme should lese the prent of the shippe in the noble and sette in the stede thereof a shepe." His dislike of the king seems to have been partly because his pocket was affected, as he "banned and cursid" the king because of the subsidy exacted from aliens; and to show his contempt for him he kept two fighting cocks, one of which he called Henry, King of England, and the other Philip, Duke of Burgundy, and he would often make them fight until Philip won. There was another alien about the same time who unwisely spoke disrespectfully of the king. This was William Turner, a Flemish tailor, who

9

came to a muster at Mile End in gaudy raiment, with silver buckles on his shoes and the arms of the Duke of Burgundy and the Bishop of " Lukys " (Liège) on his breast, and like a player or a fool played and danced about there, scheming to upset the realm. Then he went off to the Hartshorn tavern outside Aldgate, and said, " I shall drynk 100 noblys of Kyng Herry is hede of Wyndesore or Seynt George day next thanne comyng," —apparently implying that he would get the money for killing the king,—and tried to seduce his hearers from their loyalty, but finding his words unacceptable he fled to a friend's house, threw off his party-coloured dress and put on a frieze coat, but was caught.

The vivid account of his adventures at the hands of Cade's followers given in the Paston Letters by John Payn, servant of the unpopular Sir John Fastolf, is one of the best known examples of history related by an unwilling participant. I shall not repeat the details of how he saved his master's property, how he was robbed, on the point of being executed several times and finally compelled to fight for six hours in the battle on London Bridge between Cade's men and the Londoners under Matthew Gough, who had fled from Fourmigny only to fall on London Bridge, and Lord Scales, who ten years later " was slayne at Synt Mary Overeyes with watermen, and laye there dyspoylyd nakyd as a worme ; but the lordys were fulle sorry of hys dethe." Another sufferer " in the grete trobull tyme " was John Stafford, Vicar of Multon in Suffolk, whose house was broken into by a score of persons " of the affynyte of the grete traytour John Cade," who would have killed him if he had not " voyded oute of that contrey " ; as it was, he lost all his goods and dared not return to his cure. His case was, however, not so bad as that of Harry Gyllygos ten years later, who incurred the enmity of " the grete erraunt capiteyn " of Cornwall and other Lancastrian neighbours by being at Northampton when King Henry was taken prisoner. They came to his house at Helston one night, intending to hang him at his own door, but luckily he had warning and " wente oute of his bedde naked savyng his shirte," got through a window and fled to a chapel two miles off, where he stood in this scanty costume for three hours, until his clothes arrived, with the result that he caught cold, while his wife was so frightened that she " touke diverse enfirmeties that she hadd never hole day hitherto and ys never likely to have hereafter." On the Lancastrian side Thomas Gowsell got into trouble because after the battle of Tewkesbury he falsely said that King Edward had fled again to Lynn, and stirred up the people to take him and bring him to " Henrye his grete rebelle and enemye, then callyd King of England." Having been pardoned for this, he turned the accusation into profit by causing a scrivener to make a copy of the original bill against him, inserting as well the names of a number of priors and other gentry of Norfolk and naming John Skelton, esquire, as the informer. This he seems to have done partly for purposes of blackmail, but chiefly in order to disparage John Skelton and make him unpopular, but the chief result was to land himself in the Fleet. Another fellow who endeavoured to turn his own misdeeds to profit by fastening them on others was Roger Cherche, alias Bilaugh, Wryte or Bayly. About the time that Cade was up in Kent he made " a gaderyng and assemble of 15 persones in a felaschip under a wode in the town of Possewyk in Norffolk." Not content with his many aliases he determined to take a fancy name, as " Jack Straw " and " Bleweberde " had done before, and many others, including " a felowe whych renewed many of Robin Hode's pagents which named himselfe Greneleef," did afterwards. Accordingly, he " remembered a good name for her capiteyn that shuld be John Amendalle." Finding wholesale reform too large an order for his fifteen men he turned his mind to " diverse riotes, extorcons and unlaweful disheritances of gentilmen," and in order that none should " be so hardy to attempte ne lette the porposed malice of the said Roger " he caused himself to be arrested and examined by his own friends, and " imbilled dyverse gentilmen and many thrifty and sub-stancial yomen and thrifty husbondes."

As a rule, however, what the humble citizen or thrifty yeoman had to fear was not blackmail and robbery by such indirect means, but a much more direct and indiscriminate form of pillage. After the first battle of St. Albans, King Henry and his Queen failed to improve the occasion by marching on London, but " toke hyr jorney unto Yorke wardys, for they demyde that the Northeryn men wolde have ben too creuelle in robbyng yf they hadde come to London." The decision had serious consequences for the Lancastrians, for Edward of York came to London, and was received with joy by the citizens, who said, " Lette us walke in a newe wyne yerde, and lette us make us a gay garden

in the monythe of Marche with thys fayre whyte
ros and herbe, the Erle of Marche," but there is
little question that Henry was right in doubting if
he could keep his troops from plundering. That
his fear was shared by the probable victims is clear,
and amongst them a worthy brewer, William
Keynes, was much perturbed and expressed his
fears to Thomas Trebolance, " grocer otherwise
poticary beside the Standard in the Chepe."
Trebolance said that a friend of his, one Barowe
in Ludgate, had promised to protect him, and
that " upon his own dore and upon the dore of
his amite shulde be put portcolises with the name
of the said Barowe under everych of the said portcolises as servaunt to the Duc of Somerset." On
the strength, therefore, of such a portcullis painted
on Trebolance's door, Keynes entrusted his money
and jewels to the value of some £75 to the grocer,
who appears to have been as false a man as the
Duke behind whose badge he sheltered. For
after things had quieted down, whenever the good
brewer called for his money Trebolance was not
at home, and finally he took sanctuary at St.
Martins-le-Grand. His wife refused to stand trial,
and contented herself with swearing that her
husband was innocent, whereas Keynes asserted
that Thomas was " verray gilty and not innocent
as God and the said Margaret well knowe," but as
neither Margaret nor her august confederate would
reveal the truth he appealed to the Court of
Chancery, as established for " eschewyng of more
myscheves as in perjure and other many and
dyvers inconvenientes that else by the rigure and
straitnesse of the comen lawe fulle often tymes
shuld ensue."

More Medieval Byways

In support of my thesis that it is the personal note catches the public ear I might have quoted the Chitral campaign, which is remembered by nine out of ten people solely for the incident of the piper of Dargai. And he may serve as an excuse for retelling the tale of the "manly man that was a taberette." When Sir Piers de Brézé with his eighty thousand Scots fled from Norham in 1463 this gallant fellow "stode upon an hylle with hys tabyr and hys pype, taberyng and piping as merely as any man myght, standying by hymselfe; tylle my lorde of Warwycke come unto hym he wold not lesse hys grownd; and there he become my lordys man." It is satisfactory to add that till the King-Maker's death he was "with hym fulle good and to hys lorde."

II. The Medieval Boy

IT has long been my intention to write a book
on the "English Kings that Might Have
Been," the royal princes who, through their pre-
mature death or other causes, failed to ascend the
throne which should in the ordinary course of
events have fallen to their lot. The number of
them is surprising, ranging from the Conqueror's
eldest son, Robert of Normandy—for the pre-
Conquest period is too complicated, its dynasties
too evanescent, for treatment,—down to that unlucky cricketer Frederick, Prince of Wales, of
whom, " since it was only Fred, there's no more
to be said " ; in spite of which fact he has not
managed to escape the universal fate of a volumi-
nous biography. Amongst these abortive kings
are William, who perished in the White Ship, and
Stephen's two sons, that belligerent ruffian Eustace
and his inoffensive brother William. Of William,
the eldest son of Henry II, there would be little to
say, and still less of that monarch's grandson
William, whose stay on earth was confined to the
limits of a week. Whether this same William's
father, the popular star of chivalry, " the young
King " Henry, should rank as a king that might
have been, or as a king that was, is a nice problem ;
he was duly crowned, and given the title of king
in his father's lifetime ; but although to contemporaries he was Henry III, later writers have
ignored his shadowy regality, and even in the
thirteenth century there is only one chronicler who

15

persists in describing the royal opponent of Simon de Montfort as Henry IV. While there were four Williams who failed to attain the throne, there were three Edwards—the Black Prince and the sons of Henry VI and Richard III. Upon reflection, there were five Williams, if we count the little Duke of Gloucester, son to Queen Anne ; what were the names of her other children, who, like their mother, were chiefly remarkable for being dead, I cannot remember. It is rather curious that we should never have been within measurable distance of having a king with the most English of all names, Thomas, though twice an Arthur stood in the direct line, and once an Alphonso.

This Alphonso, son of Edward I, was for me, as I suppose for most people, nothing but a name, until I chanced to come upon a record of his being given a present of a little gaily painted cross-bow. Somehow this little incident makes the boy much more real to the imagination than, say, the pious moralisings of Archbishop Peckham in his letter of condolence to the King on the occasion of the death of this " hope of the nation." Alphonso's elder brother Henry was given a little cart, costing sevenpence, to play with, and also a model of a plough, which cost fourpence. Even allowing for the difference in the value and purchasing power of money at that time, the fourpence being equivalent to something like five shillings, the expense of the toys used in the royal nursery compares favourably with the cost of those expected by the ordinary modern child, as any Christmas-ridden father or conscientious uncle will admit. That the toys were strongly made we may well assume, but it is clear that they met with much the same

treatment then as now, for it was not long before
Prince Henry's cart was broken and required mend-
ing, at a cost of twopence. His mug also had to
be repaired and regilded. As for what was put
into the mug when it was mended, the accounts
show that milk was bought for the prince and his
sister, but there is also an entry of " ale bought on
many occasions for the use of the children and their
nurses." Henry being at this time in his sixth,
which was also his last, year, and his sister being
some years older, it may be assumed that they
took their share of that universal English beverage ;
but with the memory of immortal Sairey Gamp in
our minds, we may be excused for thinking that
most of it was for the benefit of the nurses, and
stood about in tall, substantial jugs on the medieval
equivalent of the " chimbley piece," so that they
might put their lips to it when they felt so dis-
poged. If such a proceeding seems too undignified
for those exalted ladies Dame Amice and Dame
Cicely, the chief nurses, it may be held to apply
to the humbler members of the royal nursery, the
rockers, such as Alice de la Grave, who was given
a pair of slippers, possibly because her own
squeaked or made too much noise. To Alice, no
doubt, fell the work of superintending the preparation of the bath on the rather rare occasions on
which the royal children indulged in such a luxury.
The bath appears to have been a quarterly affair,
mention being made of its preparation on the eves
of Christmas, Easter, and Whit-Sunday, and it
entailed something of the elaboration of a ceremonial. That it was even as frequent as this
outside the royal household may be doubted ; nor
did the Church consider that cleanliness had such

kinship to godliness as to justify any endeavour to
make the performance popular. At best the bath
was to be tolerated for reasons of health, if we may
accept the observances of the Austin Priory of
Barnwell as evidence; for they lay down the rule
that " a bath should be by no means refused to a
body when compelled thereto by the needs of ill-
health. Let it be taken without grumbling when
ordered by a physician, so that, even though a
brother be unwilling, that which ought to be done
for health may be done at the order of him who
is set over you. Should he wish for one, however,
when not advantageous, his desire is not to be
gratified." Prince Henry's Whitsun wash would
seem to have been partly, if not entirely, medicinal,
as a gallon of wine was bought for his bath; and
a later entry of payments to a man seeking herbs
throughout the neighbourhood, and purchases of
earthen pots for cooking the herbs, and of a " tan-
card " for carrying water into the chamber, suggest
the making of such a " bathe medicinable " as
that for which John Russell in the fifteenth century
gives elaborate instructions. " Holyhokke and
yardehok, peritory and the brown fenelle, walle
wort, herbe John, Sentory, rybbewort and cama-
melle, hey howe, heyriff, herbe benet, bresewort
and smallache, broke lempk, Scabiose, Bilgres,
wild flax, wethy leves and grene otes," are the
strange and complicated ingredients recommended
by Russell, and most or all of these, no doubt,
having the traditional authority of Saxon leech-
dom behind them, were tried upon the young
prince, but in vain. The boy seems to have been
ailing for some time. His elder brother, John,
had died in 1272, about the same time as his grand-

The Medieval Boy

father King Henry III, and Queen Eleanor, who was with her husband in France, had more than once written anxiously for news of the children's health. Shortly after his father's coronation, on which occasion he attended the banquet wearing a chaplet of roses and other flowers, young Henry fell seriously ill. Master Hugh of Evesham dosed him with " Letwar," " Diaboriginal," " Tria-sandal," and other mysterious concoctions ; his appetite was tempted with larks, partridges, pears, and other delicacies, but to no effect. Then the aid of the saints was invoked ; wax candles as tall as himself were sent to burn before the shrines of St. Thomas at Canterbury and St. Edward at Westminster, and also before the tomb of Henry III, as well as to the less famous altars of St. James at Reading, St. Fromund at Dunstaple, and St. Momartre outside Guildford ; but the saints proved of as little avail as the doctors, and the boy died.

In the complete absence of statistics it is impossible to get any accurate idea of the infant mortality in medieval times, but some hint of its terrible nature can be gathered from the fact that five children of Henry III died in infancy, as did four of Edward III, and no fewer than seven of Edward I. If the children of kings died off in this way the losses in humbler homes must have been great, even if we admit that the children of those parents who were too poor to employ the medieval medicine man had a better chance of surviving. If the possession of a baby is a responsibility and a cause of anxiety to a modern mother, what must it have been in those days ? The insecurity of infant life is one of the arguments advanced by a

monastic writer in favour of the adoption of the
holy and peaceful vocation of a nun. After dwell-
ing upon certain obvious disadvantages of the
married state, this upholder of the monastic ideal
continues : " there cometh from the child thus
born a wanting and a weeping that must about
midnight make thee to waken. . . . And consider his late growing up and his slow thriving, and
that thou must ever have an anxiety in looking for
the time when the child will perish and bring on
his mother sorrow upon sorrow." The logical
futility of such arguments when addressed to a
woman are proof enough that the writer was a man,
and the first sentence which I have quoted suggests
that he might himself once have been a married
man, though perhaps he spoke only from the hearsay evidence of married friends ; in any case it is
also evidence that babies have not changed greatly
during the past six or seven centuries. Boy
nature, indeed, seems to have remained much the
same ever since the days when the ungodly little
ruffians mocked at the bald and irascible prophet.
Young Lydgate, about the time that Richard II
came to the throne :

> " Ran into gardyns, applys ther I stal,
>   To gadre frutys sparyd hedge nor wal,
>   To plukke grapys in othir mennys vynes
>   Was moor reedy than for to say matynes,
>   My lust was al to scorne folk and jape,
>   To skoffe and mowe lyk a wantoun Ape."

Like the child in one of Stevenson's songs, and a
good many other children, Lydgate was " Loth to

ryse, lother to bedde at eve," regardless of the maxim of the good boy of a generation later :

> " Ryse you earely in the morning
> For it hath propertyes three,
> Holynesse, health and happy welth,
> As my Father taught mee."

Lydgate was by no means the only boy who " hadde in custom to come to scole late, nat for to lerne but for a countenaunce with my felawys, reedy to debate, to jangle and jape." The same description would seem to have applied, a century later, to Robert Barbour and Robert Fayred, who with others " accompanyed in a scole to lerne their gramer withinne the towne of Aylsham." They do not seem to have learnt " Howe to behave thy selfe in going by the streate and in the schoole," or at least they failed to follow its admirable precepts, which set forth how :

> " When to the schole thou shalte resort,
> This rule note well, I do thee exhort :
> Thy master there beyng, salute with all rever-
> ence,
> Declarynge thereby thy dutye and obedience ;
> Thy felowes salute in token of love,
> Lest of inhumanitie they shall thee reprove.
> Unto thy place appoynted for to syt,
> Streight go thou to, and thy setchel unkynt,
> Thy bokes take out, thy lesson then learne,
> Humbly thy selfe behave and governe.
> When from the schoole ye shall take your waye,
> Orderly then go ye, twoo in aray,
> Not runnynge on heapes as a swarme of bees,
> As at this day every man it nowe sees ;

Not usynge but refusynge such foolyshe toyes
As commonly are used in these dayes of boyes,
As hoopynge and halowynge as in huntynge
the foxe,
That men it hearynge deryde them with
mockes."

Had the two young Roberts borne this advice in
mind they would have spared themselves something
worse than mockery, as it befell that through their
" necligent Japyng and disport in the seid scole "
Robert Fayred received an injury of which, or at
least so his friends surmised, he " in long tyme
thereafter " died, " wherthorowghe, of grete malice
contrary to all faith trowth and conscience," the
unfortunate Barbour was thrown into prison.
Naturally it was not often that schoolboy pranks
resulted so seriously ; more often the punishment
was brief and of short duration, though painful
while it lasted. There were plenty of " tyrannical,
impatient, hare-brained schoolmasters, *Ajaces
flagelliferri*," who believed in forcing knowledge
into their scholars " by the Grecian portico," and
they were encouraged by such parents as Agnes
Paston, who expressed the hope that if her son
had not done well his master would " truly belash
him till he will amend," and put her own precepts
into practice by beating her daughter once or twice
a-week, and even breaking her head. The parents
of Lady Jane Grey expected her to do everything
" even so perfitelie as God made the world," and
if she failed to come up to their rather excessive
standard, punished her " with pinches, nippes, and
bobbes." Children in medieval England seem to
have run little risk of being spoilt through the

sparing of the rod, which was kept pretty constantly before their eyes as a deterrent, and employed behind their backs as a corrector of wickedness. The Prioress of Nuneaton in 1460, being annoyed at the intrusions of impudent boys into the convent grounds, issued general orders to her tenants that they were all to whip their children, so that in future they should not trespass within the convent precincts. Little use was it for the truant to protest or even to explain that he was late because his mother had sent him to milk the ducks !

> " My master lokith as he were madde :
> ' Wher hast thou be, thou sory ladde ? '
> ' Milked dukkis, my mother badde.'
> Hit was no mervayle thow I were sadde.
> What avaylith it me thowgh I say nay ? "

Over the master's proceedings it would perhaps be kinder to draw a veil. Suffice it to say that it was not unnatural that the boy, sore at heart,— and not only at heart,—should give vent to his feelings :

> " I wold my master were an hare,
> And all his bookis howndis were,
> And I my self a joly hontere ;
> To blowe my horn I wold not spare !
> For if he were dede I wold not care."

In these days of Montessori, when only a duke's son may be thrashed or an earl belted, and the whipping of a cook's son may lead to an action for assault, it would be rash to uphold the ancient belief that a rod " may make a chyld to lerne welle hys lesson and to be myld." Most men in these milder times incline more to the view of our duck-milking truant that " the byrchyn twyggis so sharpe " tend to make the scholar faint-hearted and to check his enthusiasm for learning, however fain he may be to become a clerk. There must have been many others than this " sory ladde " who found the attainment of the desired benefit of clergy " a strange werke " ; for in those days, when the Church and the Schools were truly demo-cratic institutions, when every cobbler's son and " beggeres brol " might become a prelate, when the butcher's son might rise to be Cardinal Archbishop and administer the affairs of the nation, when the son of a humble dependant of St. Alban's Abbey might attain the Apostolic throne and issue his orders to kings and emperors, there must have been a plenty of incompetent and unfit candidates. In the fifteenth century we find one Nicholas Glover complaining that whereas he had entrusted his son to William Bokenham, chaplain to the Clerk of the Rolls, to educate, upon the death of Master Bokenham his executor refused to give up the young John Glover to become a man of Holy Church, but intended to make him a pedlar. It is not impossible that the executor had a clearer conception of the boy's capabilities than had his father, but he might at least have combined the two professions by making him either a " par-doner," hawking pardons " come from Rome alhot," or else a " chop-church," one of those priests who raised simony to a fine art and gained their living by its practice.

The Medieval Boy

If Nicholas Glover was annoyed at his son being refused admittance to the ranks of the clergy, Thomas Taverner of Walsingham, about the same time, was equally annoyed because the prior of the Carmelites at Norwich insisted upon detaining his twelve-year-old son Alexander. There are a sufficient number of such complaints against the friars to show that they were not averse to recruiting their forces in this way, and that they were quite prepared " to take a fellow eight years old And make him swear to never kiss the girls." Their opportunities of so doing arose from the custom of entrusting children to members of religious orders for purposes of education. Although modern research has disproved the legend that in the Middle Ages all education was derived from the monks, it remains quite clear that boarders were taken and educated in many religious houses, often, no doubt, with a view to their becoming inmates, but not always. As early as 1260 John Aguillon, shortly before his death, arranged that his son Godfrey should be boarded at the little Sussex priory of Shulbred for seven years and educated to take orders of clergy ; to pay for his cost a certain rent was assigned to the priory, on condition that at the end of the seven years they should either receive Godfrey as a canon in their house or else give up the rent. The prior, however, stuck to the rent and refused to receive Godfrey. It was not, however, always the laity who got the worse of the bargain. William Patynden of Benenden sent his three sons, John, William and Thomas, to Combwell Priory " to be lerned and tought to rede and syng " by the canons, agreeing to pay eight pence a week for each of them for board and teaching. After they had been there about a year he died, owing £4 19s., which Thomasyn his widow refused to pay, although he had left her " gret substaunce of moveabilles." Similar, but still worse, was the case of Laurence Knight, gentleman, who put his daughters, Joan aged ten and Elizabeth aged seven, to school at the nunnery of Cornworthy, agreeing to pay twenty pence a week for them. The nuns appear to have been singularly long-suffering in the matter of fees, as when he died five years later he had apparently paid nothing at all, for he owed £21 13s. 4d., which his widow declined to pay.

Private tutors and governesses in some cases seem to have been employed in the houses of the greater nobles from early times, but the majority of those who possessed any book-lore—and their number was far larger than most people realise— obtained it elsewhere than in their own homes ; either at the daily grammar schools, or more rarely at boarding-schools, monastic or otherwise, and in the case of the sons of the gentry and lesser nobility, in the houses of their patrons, secular or religious. Every bishop and every great lord had in his household a certain number of boys acquiring courtesy and the rudiments of learning. As some modern writers have con-demned the loss of home influence due to the custom of sending children to school when they are eight or nine, so the Italians in 1500 con-demned the lack of affection shown by the English of the trading classes in putting their children out to strangers as apprentices at the early age of seven or eight. Whether it was due to lack of affection or not, it was certainly the fact that as the children of the middle class were sent away thus early to learn trades, so those of the upper class were sent to learn manners and all that is implied in the term courtesy. Nor can it be denied that they had much to learn, if we may judge from the various works and books of rules published for their instruction. From these same books and rhyming manuals of nurture, with their elaborate and comprehensive rules of conduct, a very good idea can be obtained both of the standard of behaviour set up as an ideal, and also of the common slips and mistakes which the uninstructed child might be expected to make. Some of the advice given is as much for all time as anything that Shakespeare ever wrote.

> " Make cleane your shoes, and combe your head,
>   And your cloathes button or lace :
>   And see at no tyme you forget
>   To wash your hands and face."

Surely there will never come a time when these simple and excellent admonitions on the subject of getting up in the morning will seem old-fashioned or out of date, although the hour of rising has moved on from " syxe of the clocke, without delay." Buttons and laces will remain perennially averse to being done up, nor will it be within the power of any reasonable child *never* to forget the bothersome process of washing. On the other hand, it should not be necessary to warn the average boy who has attained an age sufficiently advanced to be acquainted with the worthies of ancient Greece against copying one of the least pleasing habits of the most amiable and ugliest of the philosophers :

> " Nor imitate with Socrates
>   To wipe thy snivelled nose
> Upon thy cap, as he would doe,
>   Nor yet upon thy clothes."

Some of the instructions also for behaviour at table should be superfluous in a well-conducted English household ; I say English, for horrid memories of Continental hotels suggest that members of at least one great nation might well be taught in their youth some of the precepts of that good old Devonshire worthy, Hugh Rhodes ; as, for instance :

> " Burnish no bones with your teeth,
>   For that is unseemly ;
> Rend not thy meate asunder,
>   For that swarves from curtesy.
> Dip not thy meate in the Saltseller,
>   But take it with thy knyfe.
> And sup not lowde of thy Pottage,
>   No tyme in all thy lyfe.
> Defyle not thy lips with eating much,
>   As a Pigge eating draffe ;
> Eate softly and drinke mannerly,
>   Take heed you do not quaffe.
> Scratche not thy head with thy fyngers
>   When thou arte at thy meate ;
> Nor spytte you over the table boorde ;
>   See thou doest not this forget.
> Pick not thy teeth with thy knyfe
>   Nor with thy fingers ende,
> But take a stick, or some cleane thyng,
>   Then doe you not offende."

The Medieval Boy

There are other directions, such as not to throw bones under the table, and various injunctions as to the cleansing of the fingers and the handling of meat, which are now superfluous, owing to the introduction of forks, of plates, instead of trenchers of bread or of wood, and of carpets which necessitate a certain decency and restraint not always observed in the days when the floors were covered with rushes or straw. Also there are instructions for general behaviour apart from table manners ; for instance, not to claw your head or back " a fleigh as thaughe ye sought," and if spoken to by a superior not to " lumpischli caste thine head a-down, but with a sad cheer loke him in the face," or, as Richard Weste puts it :

> " Let forehead joyfull be and full,
>   It shewes a merry part,
> And cheerefulnesse in countenaunce
>   And pleasantnesse of heart.
> Nor wrinckled let thy countenance be
>   Still going to and fro :
> For that belongs to hedge-hogs right,
>   They wallow even so."

Having borrowed an image from the hedgehog, whose cousin " the fretful porpentine " Shakespeare called in aid in a famous passage, good Master Weste protests against breathing heavily " like a broken-winded horse," and continues with a triple-zoological similitude :

> " Nor practize snufflingly to speake,
>   For that doth imitate
> The brutish Storke and Elephant,
>   Yea and the wralling cat."

More Medieval Byways

The accuracy of the comparisions may be questioned, for in spite of the length of their noses it is hardly correct to speak of either the stork or the elephant as having snuffling voices. On the other hand, the unpleasantness of the cat's voice must be admitted, even if we take a more charitable view of its general character than did most medieval writers, one of whom writes as follows : " The mouse hounter or catte is an onclene beste that seeth sharpe and byteth sore and scratcheth right perylously and is a poyson enemy to all myse, and, whan she hath gotten one she playeth therwith, but yet she eteth it. And ye catte hath longe here on her mouthe, and whan her heres be gone then hath she no boldnes, and she is gladli in a warme place, and she licketh her forefete and wassheth therwith her face." No wonder, therefore, that it was forbidden at meal-times to stroke a cat or that other " onclenly beste " the dog, and that the last duty of the young gentleman-in-waiting when, in his office of chamberlain, he had seen his lord safely in bed and drawn the curtains round him was to " dryve out dogge and catte, or els geve them a clout." Having performed this office with the same zest and skill with which earlier in the day he had laid the table, waited upon his lord and possibly taken part in the complicated ceremonies of carving and serving, the youthful student of courtesy might take his leave with a low bow— " and thus may ye have a thank and reward when that ever it falle."

III. Memories ✧ ✧ ✧ ✧ ✧

" A TIME whereof the memory of man runneth not to the contrary." And a strange thing is that same memory. Not only does it perversely refuse to work at critical moments and then suddenly throw up the wished-for recollection when it has ceased to have use or interest for us, but the meshes of its net are so contrived as to let the great things slip through and retain the small. I suppose we all have minutely detailed recollections of certain utterly trivial and insignificant incidents of our childhood, and in later life the vividness and permanence of impressions bears no relation to their importance. It is this that lends value to the trivialities of the mediumistic " cross correspondences " which have in recent years led some to believe that memory can be evoked from beyond the grave. And there are curious phenomena in connection with what we may call memory, the retention of one fact or incident by association with another. Some minds are so constituted that they must be delivered of twins at every birth. They receive an impress only under a double burden and the images that they call up are all reflected. They remember that your telephone number is 1214 by the fact that Magna Charta was sealed in 1215, and can only remember that your name is Smith by recalling the fact that it is not Brown. For them was the host of *memoriæ technicæ* invented, and possibly for them was formed the German language, whose grammatical rules can only be retained by recollection of their innumerable exceptions. In one particular form almost everybody has to use this dual memory. An incident may remain vividly impressed in the mind, but if the occurrence did not touch the individual intimately it can only be dated, as a rule, by comparison with some more intimate happening. Thus we can say what time has elapsed since our friend's house was burnt by remembering that it happened just before or after we were married, while he on the other hand will know very well how long since the fire occurred but will date our marriage by its approximation to his fire. And to one who is curious of the past it is not without fascination to learn what were some of the happenings that impressed themselves most vividly upon the minds of men whose very names have been forgotten nearly half a thousand years.

Before the days of birth certificates and when parish registers did not exist the young landed proprietor who wished to get his property out of the hands of his feudal guardians had to prove that he had come to man's estate by the evidence of a dozen witnesses. In the course of such a proof of age each witness would affirm that the subject of the inquiry was born at such and such a place and date and baptised next day, as was then invariably the case, in such a church, and was therefore so old. The witness was then asked how he remembered the date after so long a lapse of time—usually twenty-two years—and the answers, showing what events had so intimately affected different persons as to constitute epochs by which they could date such an occurrence as the birth of their neighbour, throw no little light on the inner life of the people. Occasionally a cautious witness would only commit himself to the statement that it was the general opinion in the neighbourhood, amongst those who ought to know, that so-and-so was of the age of twenty-two—or whatever he might be—but as a general rule some far more definite cause of certainty was alleged. The value of the evidence varied enormously and some hearsay evidence was more weighty than other given at first hand. If little importance could be attached to the statement of a witness that he " had heard from Roger the smith," that the young squire was of full age, there was something to be said for the opinion of one whose service the child's nurse had afterwards entered. Again, John de Frompton, who asserted John Mussard's age because Dame Mussard had often recalled her son's age in conversation with him, by reason of the sufferings she sustained on account of her son, was likely to be correct, while such a first-hand witness as Randle Scot, who remembered Robert Colevill's birth because he was sitting in a tavern with some friends when the birth was announced, might well be wrong. Such evidence as that of Randle Scot, or of the four worthy men of Sussex who were sitting together in Shipley church when a friend came in and said that Edward Tregoz had just been baptised in West Grinstead, might have proved that the children had been born, but could hardly be regarded as conclusive evidence of their age.

One of the most frequent and satisfactory grounds for recollection was the coincidence, exact or approximate, of the birth of the subject with the marriage of the witness. Any man would remember the date of his wedding, without necessarily involving the implication that " he has got a wife and he knows it," and if we may disregard the old gibing retort on the man who boasted that married men live longer than bachelors, " it only seems longer,"—we may allow that a witness is not likely to err over the duration of his married life. Only a misogynist would read any evil significance into Ralph Doreward's statement that he married his wife a few days after the birth of Margaret Bovile, " and so the birth of Margaret often recurs to his memory," but there is a sinister sound about the evidence of Hugh the carpenter, who in the same year that Thomas Eyton was born married Alice, daughter of Thomas le Corveyser, " since which time he has not had a chance to forget it " (*a quo tempore nulla dies sibi datur oblivioni*). Unhappy, too, must have been John Offley's recollection of the birth of Robert Bertram of Bothal, for on the previous All Saint's Day his father married Alice, his stepmother, " and that marriage can never depart from his memory." In the proof of age of William del Isle, who was born at Pulborough the year after the Black Death, we have Richard Pigeon remembering the date because he married Joan, his wife, that year, and then we have a little light thrown on that marriage by Richard atte Mille, who recalls that in that year one Richard Pigeon went to law with his mother Joan and compelled her to marry him. It is rather a coincidence that Thomas atte Mille, of Eastbourne, remembered the birth of John Shoeswell in 1305 because in that year William du Park, of Buxted, impleaded him in Court Christian to marry his daughter. Apparently Thomas was more lucky than Joan, and escaped the forced marriage.

There is something touching about the record of William Quynteyn, who remembered the St. Clement's Eve upon which John Hawker was born, because that day he buried Theophanie his wife, whom he had only married the previous year, " and was almost mad with grief." And evil cause had one witness to remember a birth that occurred in the same year in which his own son fell into a well and was drowned, for grief at which the boy's mother was ill for half a year. Many times did witnesses recall a birth by a death. Often it was the death of a father or mother, sometimes of a child, as in the case of Benet de Refham, who remembered that at the burial of his son Hugh his dearest friend, Geoffrey de Foule-stowe of Saxilby, told him of the birth of Peter de Campania. The baptism of Bartholomew, son of John Davelers, in Erwarton church, was recalled by John Harvey because he came to the church to cause celebration to be made for his father's soul and saw the child lying in a silken cloth, and by Sir William Visdelou because that day he caused a tombstone to be placed over his father's body in the church and made a feast in honour of the event. Sometimes the circumstances of the death would have impressed it the more upon the witness's mind, as when John Bolcot's brother was " stabbed by a midnight robber," or when John Russel's son William, who had just become a monk at Boxgrave Priory, went out without leave to see his friends and was killed on the Manwode. It is something of a coincidence,—and of coincidences I shall have more to say,—that Geoffrey

Fauconer's son William, who took the vows at
Sele Priory on Whit-Sunday exactly two years
after the murder of William Russel, also went out
without leave and incurred the same penalty for
disobedience, being killed on Chanctonbury Hill.
Even more memorable was the death of the prior
of Otterton, slain by robbers who broke into
the priory the Michaelmas after William Cheyney
was born, as was duly recorded in the missal of
Upottery church.

Commonest of all comparative data, commoner
even than deaths and marriages, were the births.
Hardly a proof of age which does not contain one
such reference. As an example, the age of Geoffrey
Lucy was known in 1287 because John Mayn's
son was born the same night and Nicholas Ambroy's
daughter a few days later ; Simon Richer had a
son of the same age ; John Ward's brother Henry
was a week older and Robert le Bor's brother
William a year older than Geoffrey. One witness
had his neighbour's birth doubly impressed upon
him by his own wife presenting him with twins.
Another as he passed Danbury church saw the
infant John Chamberlain being carried out from
baptism and on reaching home found that he was
himself a father. The discovery must have been
pleasanter, and certainly less unforeseen, than that
of Simon Pyndemore, who on the day that Robert
Bertram of Bothel was born came home to find
his house in flames and lost much goods, though
he was fortunate enough not to suffer personal
injury, as did William de Hamslap, whose hand
was consumed in his endeavour to save his cattle
from fire. William Archer's birth was dated by
Thomas Rakestraw as occurring two years after

Memories

Dover was burnt by the French, which happened on August 1, 1295, at which time, according to the chronicler Fabyan, a holy man called Saint Thomas of Dover was slain. The age of John Multon of Cumberland was recalled by his having been born in 1293, in which year the city of Carlisle with the great church was burnt. But as a matter of fact it was in the previous year, 1292, that Simon de Orreton set fire to his father's house so successfully that he burnt not only it but the city with the churches of the canons and of the friars, and caused the death of nine persons, for which he was sentenced to be hanged and himself burnt.

Amongst lesser conflagrations, Roger Hilton remembered the birth of John Hawker on St. Clement's Day, 1284, because he that day gave a feast in honour of the saint, from which we may perhaps assume that he was a blacksmith, and he so overdid the roasting and the boiling and the baking that his kitchen and bakehouse were burnt down. A similar misfortune befel John of Conington when he lent his house to William Attebrok, chaplain, who baptised John Head, in order that he might hold a feast because he had then celebrated his first Mass. Feasts in themselves were memorable occasions. Twelve jurors remembered being present at Robert de Brom's marriage feast in his hall at Hartfield the year before his son John was born, and six witnesses testified that the feast given by John de Gray of Rotherfield (not, by the way, the Rotherfield which adjoins Hartfield, but that in Oxfordshire) on St. Andrew's Day, 1299, when his wife purified herself after the birth of her son, was still notorious twenty-two years later, because the abbots and priors and almost all the *probi homines* of the district—everybody in fact who was anybody—were present. These purification feasts, it may be mentioned, became so fashionable and extravagant that about 1540 the authorities at Chester prohibited them and forbade any except near relations to attend the churching of the mother and accompany her home afterwards. Not only stores of food but new dresses were in demand for the occasion, and so in 1384 when Roger Fiennes, the builder of Herstmonceux Castle, was born the Lady Elizabeth, his mother, had gowns and apparel sent out from Mayfield, that famous town where once St. Dunstan built a wooden church and pulled the Devil by the nose. So also, after the birth of John Kyriel his parents sent Alexander of Oxney across to the great manufacturing town of Ypres to buy cloth for their robes.

This Alexander of Oxney, or a namesake, some four or five years before he was sent by the Kyriels from Kent to Flanders, paid a visit to Edmund Colvill in Norfolk and saw his son Robert lying in his cradle, as he remembered two and twenty years later, in 1326, his memory being the more vivid because he gave the infant a buckle of gold. Such gifts, of ornaments, golden rings and money, were often recorded, and when Griffin, son of William de la Pole of Machynlleth, was born, his friends displayed an equally genuine but more primitive generosity, David ap Ivor giving him an ox, rather an embarrassing present for one so young, and Meredyth ap Lewellyn a cow, whose milk he may possibly have appreciated. Naturally it was the godparents who most often gave presents to the child, and it is satisfactory to find that even so early as the middle of the fifteenth century the stock godfatherly gift in the north of England was a silver mug. The names of the godparents are usually recorded in these proofs of age; they themselves often gave testimony and other witnesses often remembered incidents connected with them. When the daughter of Theobald de Verdon was baptised at Amesbury in 1317 she had no less a sponsor than Queen Isabel, and Sir John le Duyn well remembered seeing the queen come to Amesbury, while John de Harnham had a still more vivid recollection of the event as he was sub-sheriff that year and had to escort the royal virago from Clarendon. Thomas Bonvyle recalled the birth of John Paynel on Christmas Eve, 1296, because his brother came back from Flanders, where our armies were then fighting the French, and, no doubt, " swearing terribly," just in time to act as godfather. Hugh Kinder, on the other hand, who was to have acted as sponsor to Robert Mascy, turned up at Glossop church too late for the ceremony, the reason being that just as he was starting a neighbour dropped in to buy an ox, and Hugh's business instincts proved too strong for him. Whether there was any canonical rule about the age of godparents I do not know, but Walter de Ludeworth remembered the baptism of Robert de la Legh in Wearmouth church because he himself, though only nine years old, was acting as godfather to Alice, daughter of Walter Man, and Robert being christened first Alice had to wait, for which cause she wept. However, Robert did not get it all his own way, for the priest, possibly flurried by the protests of Alice, sprinkled the water on his face and eyes so excessively that

" for a long time he was angry with the said priest." But after all he came off better than little John Mitford, who, as he was being baptised in Newcastle church, fell from the chaplain's hands into the font, whereat Sir John Widdrington, his godfather, with justifiable annoyance, said to the chaplain, " Priest, priest, fond be thy head."

The proof of age of this John Mitford gives an unusually vivid picture of a christening in 1402. We see him carried to church wrapped in a beautiful fur for which his maternal grandfather, Sir Robert Lisle, had paid £5. As the party enter the church Sir Henry Percy, who happens to be passing, stops and hearing that it is William Mitford's son expresses his pleasure. Inside the church the mass of the Blessed Virgin has just been celebrated at the Holy Trinity altar, and the celebrant, hearing one of his congregation tell another who the child is, exclaims, " Thanks be to God, for now has William Mitford an heir to his name." At the font, beside the friends and relations and the clumsy priest, was a young man with a silver bason and ewer, brought from the Mitford's house, for the godparents to wash their hands after the baptism, and, although not actually mentioned in this case, there were undoubtedly others carrying torches and the salt. As they come out of the church the grandfather, Sir John Mitford, stops the nurse and says, " I ask thee, show me the child's face " ; and then he kisses him, saying, " My son, God bless thee and give thee good strength on earth."

Pleasant memories of births had those who were fortunate enough to be sent with the tidings to wealthy friends of the family. When William

Memories

Brompton, who was butler to John Davelers, told Sir Robert de Schelton of the birth of his master's son, he was rewarded with a gold ring and two shillings, while John Brown, who bore the news of Edmund Colvill's birth to his grandparents, Sir Richard de Braiose and the Lady Alice, received from them jewels worth a hundred shillings (almost as many pounds in modern money). Although not quite so lavishly rewarded, the messenger sent by John de Benstede to Lady Mary, aunt of King Edward II, at the nunnery of Amesbury, made good use of the 30s. given him, setting up with it in trade as a barber,—if barbering be a trade, a nice point which has been much argued under the Sunday Trading Act. Only one case have I noticed of a messenger being sent for a doctor to attend the mother, this being at the birth of Ralph Basset of Weldon in 1300, when a physician was fetched from Norwich to Huntingfield, a good thirty miles as the crow flies. It was in connection with a later Basset of Weldon that a romantic incident savouring of penny novelettes and transpontine melodrama occurred. In the year that Richard II ascended the throne a certain woman of the people, called Tybote Lovekyn, of Checkly, in Cheshire, bore a son, who was at once carried off by Isabel Mason to Madeley, in Shropshire, to the wife of Sir Ralph Basset who passed it off as her own. For her services Isabel received 5s. from Lady Basset; if Tybote's reward was on the same niggardly scale,—on the stage payment for supposititious heirs is always made in bags of gold,—it may account for her repenting of her share in the deception. Anyway, repent she did and confess to Thomas Broadbak, her parish chaplain, who, in spite of his name, did not care to bear the burden of responsibility and referred the case to the bishop. The bishop gave the very reasonable decision that Tybote should proclaim the facts and demand her son back, and this was done, but of what happened to Lady Basset I am ignorant.

Returning to our witnesses, we find occasionally, but far less frequently than might have been expected, that the incidents which impressed them were of historic importance. Thus Richard de Pavelly referred to the taking of Saint Louis of France by the enemies of Christ at Damietta, which happened in 1250, as occurring the year before he returned from the Holy Land. It was not inappropriate that his evidence should have been given on behalf of Fulk Fitz-Warin, third in descent, as I take it, from the famous, semi-fabulous, dragon-slaying crusader, Fulk, who after being smitten over the head with a chessboard by the youthful Prince John, in later life gave check to that king and took his knights on more than one occasion. A later King Louis figures in the proof of age of Edmund de Benstede, born in 1312, according to Nicholas de Beck, who that year was in the household of Sir Louis of France, and was sent over to arrange for his master's visit to England. The French King's visit, it may be remarked, was in anticipation of the accouchement of his sister, Queen Isabel, who on St. Brice's Day gave birth to Edward, after the Third, in honour of which event the workmen at Westminster went off work for a week, as John of Oxford, clerk of the works, well remembered. An echo of the Baron's War occurs in the case of John Musard, born at the castle of la Musardere—now wretchedly corrupted into Miserden—on the octave of St. Hilary after the siege of Kenilworth, and seen running about with his mother when Sir John Giffard came to the castle the year after Evesham—which speaks well for his precocity. The battle of Bannockburn was quoted as a date by several witnesses on behalf of Marmaduke Lumley and John de Cramlington, both of whom were born about the time of that disastrous defeat. Oddly enough, the Black Death, the terrible pestilence which swept away half the population of Europe, is mentioned scarcely at all, not do we find many references to the constant foreign expeditions of the Hundred Years' War with France, though pilgrimages—in particular St. James of Compostella—are constantly spoken of, and one Yorkshireman in 1367 anticipated his later compatriots by going to the Isle of Man. Prior to this little trip he took leave of his neighbours in the church of Bolton Percy—where, as it happened, Margaret Chaumont was being baptised :—*cepit licenciam de vicinis suis* is the choice piece of latinity, to which we feel inclined to append, instead of an expostulatory (*sic*) the more forcible protest of (*bow wow*).

Accidents, and in particular broken limbs, figure largely in our records, but rarely can there have been such a crop of fractures as occurred in London at the birth of Ann Payn. On the day that she was baptised John French, brewer's man, carrying a kilderkin of ale on his shoulder, fell and broke his left leg ; John Dover, a carpenter, was blown off the roof of a house in St. Peter's, Cornhill, and broke an arm, as did also John Colton, tiler ; Alan Rous, mason, building a wall at St. Austin's, fell and broke his ribs, from which he died ; and Edward Holderness, a sailor, coming up from Stratford, dropped dead in the road outside Aldgate. Natural phenomena, too, are not absent. Twelve witnesses testified that Philip Staunton was born in the year that a thunderbolt shattered the castle of Roch, in Pembrokeshire, and it must surely have been the same appropriate agency by which the church and parsonage of Thunderley were burnt down at Christmas, 1291, so that for six years all services had to be held in the manor chapel. Immediately after the baptism of Henry Fenwick in 1401 "so great and strong a wind arose that all the men and women of the vill greatly feared for the shaking of their frail houses," and when Robert Gatefore was born in 1421 there was such heavy rain that the Tyne rose and flooded John Rae's house in Newcastle.

It is a little disconcerting to find that there was an exactly identical wind after the baptism of Thomas Lumley in 1408 and a precisely similar flood in John Rae's house when John Orde was born in 1423. The theory of coincidences is rather strained when we find witnesses in different parts of Essex remembering four different births because (1) John Waryn hanged himself at Great Teye ; (2) John Wargon hanged himself at Little Laver ; (3) John Wareyn hanged himself at Thorpe ; and (4) John Warde hanged himself at Layer Marny. When we find, moreover, that in each case one witness fell off a haycart and broke his left arm and another broke his left leg playing football we cannot help doubting their accuracy, and no amount of explanation will render it probable that Robert

Memories

de Milneburne's father died both on March 24, 1307, when Robert Bertram was born, and also on Februrary 1, 1308, when David de Strabolgi was born. It is clear that some of the evidence must be false, and the worst of it is that it all sounds so plausible. As proof of the age of Isabel Hathewy in 1382 we read that in the year she was born the parishioners of Ruwardyn bought an image of the Blessed Virgin, which is still in the church ; three witnesses declare that on that day they began to lay the foundations of the belfry, and another recollects that on the same Sunday the parishioners decided to buy a new missal. All very circumstantial and convincing, but you find it all word for word in the proof of age of William Bulneys, except that the church is that of Sibthorpe, Notts. Again, when John Bigod was born Joan Barneston, the midwife, told William Malet that the mother " had got a beautiful boy " ; Joan Shefferd, midwife, also spoke of " a beautiful boy " when Robert Blount was born in London. Nothing remarkable about that ; nurses have been making that same remark for centuries and will continue to do so. But when we find that the midwife who described Hugh Lowther of that ilk, born in distant Westmoreland, as " a beautiful boy " was also called Joan Shefferd—well, " I don't believe there's no sich person."

As to how much of all this evidence is true and how much false and why on earth it should have been necessary to display so much perverse ingenuity in inventing evidence it is difficult to say anything definite. Probably in each case the first occurrence is genuine, but it would be rash to dogmatise. "All men are liars," and all have not the self-restraint of the servant who told her mistress indignantly that she "never told unnecessary lies."

IV.   Deceivers Ever

" LOVE'S limits are ample and great ; and a spatious walk it hath, beset with thorns, not lightly to be passed over."   And whether love be, as some theosophical mystics would have us believe, the affinity of twin reincarnations, or whether it be, on the other hand, a mere matter of chromosomes and a development of instincts innate in the " primordial protoplasmic globule," our ultimate ancestor, it certainly is not lightly to be passed over.   History has shown not once or twice " how easily the world may burn when kings come out a-wooing," and if the love affairs of lesser mortals kindle correspondingly smaller conflagrations they yield the unfortunate victims a sufficiently hot time none the less.   From the day when Eve wooed Adam with an apple to the November night when that " bigge damsell "— and forward hussey—Anne Holden, aged twelve, enticed James Ballard, her junior by a year, with two apples to come and get married at the un-canonical hour of ten, when they ought both to have been in their beds, love has got our forebears into trouble.   Nor is it a matter in which the experience of others avails the sufferer.   Little use for him to reflect philosophically with the old fisherman that " women are like pilchards, when they'se good they'se only middlin', and when they'se bad they just be bad."   It may be true enough that " if women in generall be so bad, and men worse than they, what a hazard is it to

47

marry!" Yet who has ever been turned from
the path of matrimony by such second-hand
wisdom? None so blind as Love, for he refuses
to see, and even when he sees it makes little
difference. William Hoddesdon of Harrow, who
lived in the days of the much-married Henry VIII,
of dread memory, was under no illusions as to the
virtues of Joan Bradley,—or at least he had lost
most of them, to judge from his language, before
he had finished with her, but still wished to yoke
himself to her. His case was the more remarkable
in that he was a widower and "as the comicall
poet merrily saith, '*Perdatur ille pessime qui
foeminam Duxit secundus*'"; it was indeed some
of his first wife's stuff that he bestowed upon the
fickle Joan, adding thereto a "payre of coral
bedes," or a rosary, which I fear she regarded
rather as an adornment than a means of grace,
when he was formally betrothed to her. But when
he returned to Kensington, "for to have been
maryed," he found that Joan had gone off with
one Fayrefoote to London. Thither he followed
her, tracing her as far as St. Katherine's by the
Tower, only to discover that she was betrothed
to "an olde man, a maryner." Slightly disconcerted by the discovery of this third claimant for
her hand, William returned to Kensington and
sought the advice of Master Meawtys, presumably
the family lawyer. This worthy man of law
reassured him as to his claim upon the faithless
Joan and recommended him to get the constable
to break open the door of her house; the deed
was done and he slept there several nights, "lowk-
yng alwayes when she wolde com to perfourme
her promesse." But when the bird returned not

to her nest, he called in the constable and some neighbours to take an inventory of her goods and carted half of them off to Harrow, still protesting that he would marry her in spite of all that had happened—to paraphrase into printable mildness his vigorous characterisation of her conduct. The lover in this case got off easily, for not only did he avoid marrying the woman, for which good fortune he was not duly grateful, but he secured half her goods; the unfortunate constable and neighbours, however, suffered for their share in the adventure, for Joan, by the support of one Hamlet, " the kynges carttaker,"—probably her latest love,—had some of them arrested and carried off to the Marshalsea. One of her victims was " fayne to cause his wif to ley hir beste gowne to plege " that he might pay the necessary fees to the prison officers, " or els they wold have had his cote from hym to his utter undowyng." To some extent it may restore our opinion of women to find a wife willing to sacrifice her gown, even her best gown, to save her husband's coat.

If the course of true love never did run smooth, the way of the offender was equally liable to prove rough—particularly so when he had omitted to get off with the old love before getting on with the new. Not such an easy job, either, to get off with the old love in those days, when a betrothal was as valid and binding as a marriage. When once the man had said, " I Will sall wed thee, Janet, at ye kirk-dore," and she had replied, " Will'm, I sall never hafe housbande bot thee Will'm whilles ye live "—or words to that effect— there was no escape. Least of all could the bonds of one contract be broken by forming a second, as

many a man found to his cost. In fact this only
introduced fresh complications, as Anthony Hourde
realised when he got engaged first to Janet Armstrong and then to Marian Martin. Marian
declined either to release him or to abide by the
decision of friendly arbitrators, but vowed to take
the law on him " for discharge of her sowle," and
if Janet was one of the Armstrongs of the Dales
he would have been a rash man who scorned her,
while if she was the same Janet who some years
later got into trouble for saying that a neighbour
had " murdered and put down his two wyfes " it
is to be feared that her tongue would have made
her as dangerous married as scorned. Nor does
there seem to have been any statute of limitations
to help the shifty lover. Janet Ferry claimed
Martin Highe as her husband fourteen years after
the momentous Sunday upon which they " dyd
pleight ther faith and trueth to the other as man
and wyff by for God, after the contry maner,"
upon which occasion they were handfasted by
Janet's grandfather, Lancelot Ettes, who was
evidently not only " a very elderly man," but also
a tedious old proser, for he " sayd so moch there-
upon that one might have goon a mile in the space."
Even the refuge of religion was denied the repen-
tant suitor, and when William le Ferour sought to
escape by taking the vows as a canon of Merton
Priory Julia Vyne followed him up all the way
from York and claimed him for her own. Margaret
Snede was another young woman who displayed a
persistent energy in claiming her rights ; although
when she sued Thomas Gylberd, a London inn-
keeper, before Dr. Wharton, the Bishop's Chancellor, she was not successful in compelling him to

marry her, she returned to the attack, and on the very day before he was to be married to another woman, Margaret, " not content with her uncharitabill vexacon," as Gylberd put it, haled him again before the chancellor. Somehow or other Margaret so worked upon that highly susceptible chancellor that he ordered the unlucky Tom to pay her £10, and caused him " maugry his hedde " to seal an obligation for that amount, sending him round for that purpose to a scrivener's under escort of a servant " with a sworde and a bokeler and a dager."

It was not always the man who was fickle in those days, whatever may be the case now, and the woman's exercise of her immemorial privilege of changing her mind not infrequently led to trouble. Of course there are two sides to every question, and a great many more than two where a woman is concerned, and possibly Agnes Raphaels was right when she utterly denied that she had engaged herself to Hugh Oversall, of Hull, mariner, when she was a widow and before she married Robert Raphaels. The sailor, however, " sweir grete othys that he and the said Agnes were handfast," and either because her own conscience smote her or because Hugh was " a Powler and without any conscience " she compromised and although she would not give herself to him allowed him to take " a last of mutton talowe, which as then was worthe 12^{li} of Englishe money and bettur." Even this unromantic substitute for a wife she endeavoured to deprive him of when once she was safely married. Another case of a fickle woman and certain " powlers "—this time on her side—occurred when William Norreys espoused Alison

Lacy on the strength of certain money left to her by her father and the promise of a further 20 marks from her brother, John Lacy, rector of Chilton. William, as becomes a suitor, gave her many "yeftes," to the value in his own estimation of 100s., and then Alison and her brother turned nasty, and he could neither get the girl nor her money nor his gifts. Moreover, the rector "gederid unto him at Oxenford in riotous maner to the nombre of 24 persones, Powlers, araied in forme of war," and opposed the unlucky William so that "he myght not passe out of the towne, but through grete daunger unslayn." The appearance of all these "powlers," or "pollers" to use the more usual spelling, at Oxford suggests an unkind inquiry as to the possible connection of this word, which implies an idle, rowdy fellow, with poll degrees.

In this Oxford case the complaining suitor frankly admits that he was after the young lady's property, and the maxim that "Cupid in all his amorous battles, No advantage finds like goods and chattels," is exemplified over and over again in these old matrimonial cases. It was, of course, the prospect of worldly advantage that led to the practice of infant marriage, a practice which continued well into the reign of good Queen Bess. That infants should be carried to church and made to lisp the words of the marriage service and a refractory bridegroom bidden to repeat a little more and then run away and play may seem absurd, but unless the husband and wife repudiated the marriage when they attained that age of discretion at which the modern boy is usually just entering a public school the contract was binding.

Deceivers Ever

In that lay its advantage over the mere agreement of marriage, as Thomas Thorisby, merchant of Lynn, may have realised. He, it seems, had arranged for his daughter Margery to marry Harry, son of John Pagrave, gentleman, the bridegroom's gentility being counterbalanced by the bride's dower of £100. Half of this dower the worthy merchant paid down, John Pagrave in return handing Harry over to his intended father-in-law, by whom he was placed at the grammar-school in Lynn. Six months later John Pagrave sent a messenger to Lynn, and " desired the scolemaister of the said scole to have the said Herry into the towne to drynke with a kynsman of his " (the fifteenth century equivalent of going out to tea, which in its turn may sound shocking dissipation to our descendants five centuries hence)—and spirited him away, leaving Margery to lament a suitor and her father the less easily replaced £50.

It is to be feared that many deceitful men endeavoured to pluck the flower profit out of the nettle matrimony without incurring its responsibilities. Margaret Appelgarth was not the only woman in the sixth Henry's days who thought that her suitor was speaking " ful sadly and hertly " when he protested his love for her and, on the strength of it, borrowed money which, unlike his promises, he kept. Then there was the case of Cecily Bannyng, a Wiltshire serving lass, whose master, William Woodman, was so pleased with her diligence that he promised to marry her, and she " did the more diligently her service and more fayne and glad to please him " (there is something to be said for making love to your cook), and, not suspecting that he " entendid falsehed crafte and

sotelty," even left in his hands 40s. in money and
" certayn napre as shetes borde clothes, towells
and kerchiefs." Woodman threw her over and
stuck to her goods, and the sad part of it was that
she had "forsakyn dyverse persons which have
made instant labour to hir and also to hir frendes
to have her in mariage, to her great hurte, losse,
hynderaunce and in maner undoyng forever."

If some men have at times used Cupid as a go-
between to negotiate their loans and not always
discharged the debts incurred in his name, it is
only fair to point out that more frequently love
has led to an unwonted, and sometimes unwise,
generosity. The exchange of tokens, more especially of rings or of the "bowed groat," which was
the medieval equivalent of the "crookit bawbee,"
has always been almost an essential of an engage-
ment, and he was a poor lover who did not add
further substantial proofs of his affection in the
shape of presents. This entirely laudable custom
occasionally led to unpleasantness when the lady
tired of her lover but retained her affection for his
presents. John Patche, for instance, having lived
three centuries too early to profit by the elder
Weller's caution as to widows, trusted the "wordis
of grete comforte to marye with hym" with which
Eleanor Weldon, widow, of Southwark, encouraged
him and bestowed upon her "peces of gold and
other tokyns to the some of 46s. 8d.," but found
that she would neither fulfil her "comfortable
wordis and promise" nor return the tokens. So
with that worthy Staffordshire gentleman, Mr.
Richard Cotton, when he was courting Alice Eyton,
of Shropshire, in the days before bluff King Hal
had tired of his first queen. He gave her a ser-

geant's ring,—a plain gold band like the modern wedding-ring, but usually engraved with a " posy," and taking its name from the custom by which sergeants-at-law presented such rings to the Chancellor on their appointment,—" a ringe with a Turkise, a tablett of gold, a crymesyn gyrdell wovyn like a call (*i.e.*, a caul or web), a hoke of silver and gilt brodered with perells," but because at the time when he made these various presents he did not stipulate for their return if the marriage were broken off,—and what lover could act in so cold-blooded a fashion?—therefore he could not get back his jewellery. Then there was John James who, after a flirtation with Mistress Gray, set his affections on Elizabeth Morgan and gave her " a rynge of gold with a dyamant, a ryng of gold set with certen stones, lyke to a dragones hede, a ryng of gold called a serjauntes ryng, a crosse of gold with a crucyfysse, thre pomaunders, a rebon of sylke, a pyncase of cloth of gold," and other tokens; and then she went and married John Maurice! That at least was his version, but Elizabeth declared that when he proposed she told him to " ask Papa," or, in her own words, " that he shuld fyrst prove her fadur,"—a medieval custom which, I gather, has been abolished by the present generation. Her father refusing his consent she would have nothing to do with him, and though it was true he sent her presents she refused them and some of them she " cast into his sleve and he cast them out upon the ground," and she was quite ready to return them at any time. Our sympathy may well be on the lady's side in the case of Elizabeth Repynton, " a poore mayden havyng fewe fryndes but oonely the grace of God and her poore mother " (which is reminiscent of the old dame who would have been drowned if it had not been for " Providence and another woman "). William Myrrell, a Bristol merchant, had betrothed himself to her by gifts of " a grete crusadoo of gold to the value of 45s. and two fyne kerchers to the valewe of 3s.," but he having died before the wedding his executors " of there covetous mynde " laid claim to the " crusadoo " and the kerchiefs. On the other hand, it was very hard on John Aguillam, King's sergeant-at-arms, to have bestowed upon Margaret Ramsey, widow (oh, those widows !), goods and tokens to the value of £40, which she " thankfully resceyved of hym and the same yet reteyneth and keepith to her own use and thuse of Richard Restwold nowe hir husband." To feel that he was benefiting his rival and supplanter must have been galling, and it is no wonder that John was " gretly trobilled and vexed to his great hurt and damage." Galling too must have been Elizabeth Bedcotte's retort when John Ashe brought an action for breach of promise against her, complaining that for her sake he had made " many longe and idle jorneyes unto her, and therby to forslowe his trade unto his veary great losse," and had also given her presents worth £20. She admitted that he had been her suitor, but as for his presents, well, he gave her " a paire of gloves not worth above 8d., and dyd send her for a fayring a little hoopte rynge gylded uppon som white mettle but whether yt be uppon sylver, tynne or pewter she cannot tell,"—anyhow it was not worth more than 2s. Beyond that he gave her nothing but—*honi soit qui mal y pense*—a garter worth some sixpence. Moreover,—final touch of contempt,—she considered she was quite justified in refusing to marry a fellow who made such a fuss about so little. And so "Much Ado About Nothing" ended in "Love's Labour Lost."

A notable difference between the medieval and the modern breach of promise action is that whereas the modern plantiff or her counsel (I say "her," for nowadays men dare not bring such actions against the fair sex) claims damages for the mental anguish endured, and pretends to scorn the more material question of expenses incurred, the plaintiffs of earlier days addressed themselves to the recovery of money or goods bestowed upon the beloved and laid no claim to recompense for broken hearts. The only instance that occurs to me of a demand for "moral and intellectual damages" was made not on behalf of the forsaken damsel but on behalf of her guardian. It seems that in 1469, while he was studying law up at Cambridge, Richard Narborough fell in love,—a not infrequent occurrence in that home of learning, as some of us can testify. His beloved was Lucy Brampston, daughter-in-law of a local physician, Walter Leinster, and Master Richard before leaving England for a two years' course at the famed university of Padua had an interview with Dr. Leinster, and requested him to take care of Lucy and her maid during his absence, promising that on his return in two years' time he would marry her and pay the cost of her maintenance. Time passed ; the two years lengthened out to three and four, but still Richard returned not. Filled with a zest for knowledge, or fear of his affianced, he wandered from Padua to Louvaine, Bruges and Ghent, but did not turn his steps towards Cambridge. He disregarded all messages, loving or admonitory, sent by the hands of the Archdeacon of Norfolk or Master Edmund Wright or others and ignored the faithful Lucy, who fell into " a sore and gret sekenes causid thrugh his onkyndnes and chaungeablenes, ful hard to escape with lyiffe, as al the cuntrey knowith wel, as yet apperith on hir, for ever sith she hath ben sekele thrugh sorowe and pensyffenes which she toke for his new-fangles." At last, after ten years, Richard, now a full-blown Doctor of Civil Law, returned to London, where he was at once tackled by the persistent Dr. Leinster. An interview with the patient Lucy failed to rekindle his love, and Dr. Narborough declined to marry her or to repay the 130 marks due for the board and lodging of herself and her maid at the reasonable rate of 3s. 4d. the week. Nor would he even discharge the ten years' arrears of her modest dress allowance of two pounds " yerely delivered to her to buy gownys, kirtells, smokkis, etc." In fact, he completely repudiated his contract, to the injury of Dr. Leinster's pocket, and the great peril and jeopardy of his own soul. The answer to the question " When doctors disagree who shall decide ? " was, in this case—the Lord Chancellor. Before him, therefore, Dr. Leinster laid his case, setting out in detail the expenses he had incurred and adding at the end : " For myn interest and grevous trowble in al the tyme and space of the said 10 yere, whiche God knowyth yef I myght a chosen I wolde not a suffrid for the wynning of £300 and more, I remit to your noble wisdome," thus leaving the assessment of moral damages to the Chancellor, but with an ingeniously inserted hint that they should be at

Deceivers Ever

least £300. Unfortunately, like the "story of Cambuscan bold," our tale is left half told; we have neither Dr. Narborough's version nor the Chancellor's decree, and we are therefore unable to say how the Chancellor dealt with the doctors.

V. Medieval Cookery   ❧   ❧   ❧

"WHAT an Hodg-potch do men that have
    Abilities make in their Stomachs, which
must wonderfully oppress and distract Nature.
For if you should take Flesh of various sorts, Fish
of as many, Cabbages, Parsneps, Potatoes, Mustard, Butter, Cheese, a Pudden that contains more
than ten several ingredients, Tarts, Sweetmeats,
Custards, and add to these Cherries, Plums, Cur-
rans, Apples, Capers, Olives, Anchovies, Mangoes,
Caveare, &c., and jumble them together into one
Mass, what eye would not loath, what Stomach
not abhor, such a Gallemaufrey ?   Yet this is done
every Day, and counted Gallent Entertainment."

Probably most people imagine that the indiscriminate consumption of every kind of fish, flesh,
fowl, fruit, and vegetable, and the concoction of
savoury messes, and " puddens " of multiple ingredients, is an abuse of modern luxury unknown
to our hardy ancestors.   That Lucullus and other
ancient Romans had brought the art of cookery to
an unsurpassed height is, of course, a matter of
more than common knowledge, and no reputation
for erudition can be obtained, even at a suburban
dinner-party, by references to dishes of nightingales' tongues or to the emperor who ransacked the
known world that he might feast on phœnix before
he died.   But when it comes to medieval times
there is a prevalent idea that our English ancestors
were gross rather than elaborate eaters ; oxen and
sheep roasted whole, an occasional boar's head at

Medieval Cookery

Christmas, perhaps a swan or a peacock at a nobleman's board, and, of course, a venison pasty,—such would be the popular idea of a medieval menu, and if puddings were suggested it is probable that hesitating votes would be cast for something solid in the suet-pudding line. It is also not uncommon to hear complaints that the poorness of modern teeth may be traced to the newfangled custom of eating soft and overcooked foods, and to such innovations as stews and fricassées. Now it is quite true that our ancestors did eat on a large scale, and that their preparations for a feast were apt to be wholesale and even Gargantuan. The provisions for King Richard II and the Duke of Lancaster, when they dined with the Bishop of Durham in London in September, 1387, suggest the victualling of a town against a siege. What the number of their united retinues may have been I do not know, but they should have fared pretty well with 120 sheep, 14 salted and 2 fresh oxen, 140 pigs and 12 boars, 210 geese, 720 hens, besides 50 capons " of hie grece " and 8 dozen other capons, 50 swans and 100 dozen pigeons, a few odd scores of such things as rabbits and curlews, with corresponding quantities of accessories, as eleven thousand eggs, 120 gallons of milk, and 12 gallons of cream. By way of comparison I have jotted down the orders given for articles of food to be sent to the court of Henry III for Christmas in 1246 ; they include five thousand chickens, eleven hundred partridges and as many hares and rabbits, ten thousand eels, 36 swans, 54 peacocks, and 90 boars,—these latter expressly specified as being " with their heads whole and neatly carved," an important stipulation, as

More Medieval Byways

> " The boar's head, I understonde,
> Is first service in the londe
> Whersoere it can be found.
> *Servitur cum sinapio.*"

Brawn and mustard, indeed, was the stock form of
hors-d'œuvres with which every banquet opened,—
so much so that it even figured at the head of the
wonderful fish dinner given by Henry V at the
time of his marriage to gentle Kate of France,—
and the boar's head was only the exalted form of
the humble brawn which, we learn, might grace
the peasant's board, for

> " A Franklen may make a feste improberabille :
> Brawne with mustarde is concordable,
> Bakon served with peson."

If anywhere, we should expect to find in a
franklin's feast solid and substantial fare, and it is
true that beef or mutton, chicken, goose and
pigeon, apples and pears, " with bred and chese to
calle," do figure in the list ; but with them we also
find " custade," which has nothing to do with our
custard, but is really a " crustade " or pasty,
" jusselle," " dowcettes," " frytours and a leche
lovely," spiced cakes and wafers, washed down
with mead and the similar, uninviting liquor,
" bragot." Of these, a " leche " is a sweet of the
same sort of vague and varying composition as
what is now called a shape or mould ; jussell is
more in the nature of a savoury—to make it you
take eggs and bread-crumbs, and " swyng them
togydere," add sage and parsley, salt and saffron,
cook it in good broth but strain it off and let it get

solid before serving. Doucettes appear to have been a kind of sweet pork pie, judging from the recipe, which runs as follows : " Take Porke and hakke it smal, and Eyroun (= eggs) y-mellyd togederys and a lytel Milke, and melle hem togederys with Hony and Pepir and bake hem in a cofyn (= a pie crust), and serve forth." Like most fifteenth-century recipes this carries a suggestion of vigour which makes one feel that the cook in those days must have been a person of muscle and energy ; to do jugged hares he is bidden first to " hacke hem in gobettys," while for " pigge in sauge " the directions are : " Take a pigge, draw him, smyte off his hede, kutte him in iiij quarters, boyle him til he be ynow, take him uppe and lete cole, smyte him in peces," and after seasoning, " cowche thi pigge in disshes and caste the sirippe theruppon."

If we find a certain elaboration in the cookery of the farmer's household, we may expect, or even assume, further refinements and complications at the tables of the wealthy ; and so far is it from a fact that kickshaw cookery, to the deterioriation of teeth and morals, is a modern innovation, that four centuries ago a rhyming moralist protested alliteratively against the abuse.

Cookes with theire newe conceytes, choppynge, stampynge and gryndynge,
Many newe curies all daye they are contryvynge and fyndynge
That provokethe the peple to perelles of passage throug peyne soore pyndynge,
And throug nice excesse of suche receyttes of the life to make an endynge.

" Some with Sireppis, Sawces, Sewes and Soppes,
   Comedies, Cawdelles cast in Cawdrons, pannes and
     pottes
   Leeses, Jelies, Fruturs, Fried mete that stoppes
   And distempereth alle the body, both bak, bely and
     roppes."

No doubt it was right and wise to issue such
warnings, " lest the belly-god hale you at length
captive into his prison-house of gurmandise, where
you shall be afflicted with as many diseases as you
have devoured dishes of sundry sorts " ; but while
it is true enough that " God may sende a man
good meate, but the devyll may sende an evyll
coke to dystroye it," yet there is something to be
said for the counter-proverb, " A good Cooke can
make you good meate of a whetstone." In many
cases the cook must have had poor material to deal
with, and much skill must have been required to
render the results appetising. One of the cleverest
of medieval doctors declared that " A good coke is
halfe a physycyon, for the chefe physycke (the
counceyll of a physycyon excepte), dothe come
from the kytchyn," adding that—" yf the physycyon, without the coke, prepare any meate,
excepte he be very experte, he wyll make a
werysshe dysshe of meate the whiche the sycke
can not take." At the same time it would be
unwise for any enthusiastic admirer of ancient times
and methods to put into the hands of his cook the
recipe-book of a fifteenth-century predecessor of
Hannah Glasse (of hare-catching fame), or the
omniscient Mrs. Beeton. (In parentheses, what a
magnificent piece of irony would it have been if
Mr. Beeton had been a confirmed dyspeptic or a

Medieval Cookery

convinced vegetarian;—only a Greek tragedian
or Colonel Newnham-Davis could deal with
such a theme as it deserves.) What cook,
even if her board-school education had been
supplemented by a course of cookery classes at a
technical school, could deal satisfactorily with this
recipe for " Daryoles " ?—" Take croddys of the
deye and wryng out the whey ; and take yolkys of
Eyroun, nowt to fewe ne nogt to many, and strayne
hem bothe togederys thorw a straynour, and than
hard thine cofynne and ley thine marew ther-in ;
and pore thine comade theron, and bake hem and
serve hem forth." The " yolkys " might betray
the identity of " Eyroun " with eggs and the
mention of whey might suggest that " croddys "
were curds, but it is probable that the connection
of the qualifying " deye " with dairy would defeat
her ; nor could she be expected to recognise
" marew " as being marrow, and " comade " as
referring to the strained eggs. As to " hard thine
cofynne," my difficulty is the opposite of the
cook's ; I know what it means, but do not know
the modern terms : the " cofynne," which is to be
baked, is the pastry casing into which the mixture
is to be put. Even when interpreted, most of
these recipes would exasperate a modern cook by
their omission of all mention of quantities. That
just quoted is almost unusually exact in saying
that the eggs must be not too many nor too few.
Opening the book casually my eye is caught by
" Papyns " ; for this dish you are told to " take
fayre mylke and floure . . . take yolkys of eyroun
. . . take sugre, a gode quantityte, . . . a lytil
salt . . . sette it on the fyre tyl it be sumwhat
thikke," directions which certainly err on the side

5   65

of vagueness. Some of the names also tend to confusion : " Blamang" proves to be a mixture of chicken and rice and almonds ; " Charlette " has nothing to do with either Apple Charlotte or Charlotte Russe, but is made of little bits of veal or pork boiled with eggs and ale ; and " Sardeynes " are not the little headless savouries whose identity has been disputed in the Law Courts, but a compound of rice and spice and sugar and milk. Some of the names would ornament the card of fare, even if the concoctions themselves were not satisfactory to a modern palate : " Blandyssorye," " Egredoucye," " Mammenye," " Arbolettys," and " Crustade gentyle " sound inviting ; " Flathons," " Flampoyntes," " Chawettys," " Hanoneye," and " Pocerounce " have at least the charm of the unknown ; but it might be as well not to put " Garbage " on the menu without a footnote to explain that this was merely the old name for giblets.

A Tudor invention the menu, if we may believe Harrison, who says that the clerk of the kitchen " useth (by a tricke taken up of late) to give in a breefe rehearsall of such and so many dishes as are to come in at everie course throughout the whole service in the dinner or supper while : which bill some call a memoriall other a billet but some a fillet, bicause such are commonly hanged on a file." For earlier times, therefore, we are more fortunate than the contemporary diners, as we possess the menus of quite a large number of public dinners, such as the coronation banquets of Henry IV and Henry VI, the installation feasts of several prelates, and so forth. If we have to " dine with Duke Humphrey " in the proverbial sense of having nothing to eat, we can at least regale ourselves in imagination at the good Duke's table, picking our way through the three courses from the inevitable mustard and brawn down to the "quince bake, leche dugard, and fruture sage," ending up with "Blaunderells or pepyns, with caraway in confite; waffurs to ete, ypocras to drynk with delite." That three courses should be the normal length of a public dinner might seem to support the theory that our ancestors were wiser than we, especially as there is never any mention of the speeches which now prolong the boredom of similar entertainments. As a matter of fact, however, each course was a dinner in itself, and included the most varied assortment of dishes. At Duke Humphrey's table the first course was composed of soup, beef and mutton, swan, pheasant, capon, venison bake, etc.; the second contained two soups or pottages, "blanger mangere," birds, including peacock "in hakille ryally"— that is to say, with all its feathers on, "rabettes sowkere" (sucking rabbits were a favourite dainty), "dowcettes, payne puff and leche Jely Ambere"; and the third, cream of almonds, small birds such as snipe, quails, and "mertinettes rost," fish, such as perch in jelly and freshwater crayfish, and various sweetmeats. Such confusion of substance was typical of the normal three courses, and it is difficult to see why the triple division should have been considered necessary, unless it was to afford opportunities for the display of artistic ingenuity in the making of the "subtleties" with which each course was distinguished. These "subtleties" were more or less elaborate devices worked in pastry, sugar and jelly representing figures or scenes appropriate to the occasion. The pudding in the shape of a lion which Martha set before Miss Matty, and which the latter declared ought to be put under a glass shade (I trust all my readers know their " Cranford " well enough to remember the incident), was a humble " subtlety." At the wedding of Henry V two of the " soteltes " took the form of figures of St. Katherine, in allusion to the royal bride ; those at the installation banquet of Archbishop John Stafford depicted the Holy Trinity with St. Thomas of Canterbury, St. John the Baptist, and other saints ; while at Archbishop Warham's feast one represented the interior of an abbey church ; that suggested for a model " Feste for a bryde," or wedding breakfast, in the sixteenth century was certainly appropriate, if a little previous.

There were not wanting protests against all this miscellaneous feeding and pleas for method as well as for moderation. Old Burton, quoting Crato, declares : " It much availes likewise to keep good order in our diet, to eat liquid things first, broaths, fish, and such meats as are sooner corrupted in the stomach ; harder meats of digestion must come last." A century before Burton wrote Andrew Borde had complained that " Englysshe men hath an evyll use ; for at the beginning at dyner and supper he wull fede on grose meates, and the beste meates which be holsome and nutratyve and lyght of dygestion is kept for servauntes ; for whan the good meate doth come to the table, thorowe fedynge upon grose meate the appetyde is extynct." The same writer is one of the earliest authorities for the use of olives as *hors-d'œuvres :* " Olyves condyted, and eaten at the begynnynge of a re-

fectyon, doth corroborate the stomacke and pro-
voketh appetyde." He pays a similar testimony
to capers and also says that " six or seven damy-
sens eaten before dyner be good to provoke a mans
appetyde ; the skyn and the stones must be abla-
tyd and caste awaye and not used." In the matter
of soups the ordinary pottage was more in the
nature of a broth or even a stew, and made up in
body what it lacked in clarity, but where fish were
concerned, our ancestors had a far wider range of
choice than we. At the great fish banquet given
by Henry V in honour of his wedding no fewer than
forty varieties of fish were served, ranging from
whale to minnows. If any purist objects that
whale is not a fish, I will concede him the scientific
point and fall back upon the infallible authority
of the Pope, for the Church undoubtedly held that
whales and everything else that moved in the
waters were fish, some flesh-loving casuists even
endeavouring to include in Lenten fare the beaver's
tail, which one writer classes with salt porpoise
and seal as " deynteithes fulle dere." It must
have been their meatiness rather than any delicacy
of flavouring which brought into favour such
apparently unattractive fish as the whale, seal,
porpoise,—" the which kynde of fysshe is nother
praysed in the olde testament nor in physycke,"—
and sturgeon. The latter, always eaten with
whelks, which are possibly not so repellent as their
appearance on barrows in the smaller streets of
London would lead one to suppose, was notoriously
a royal fish, and the abundance of orders for slices
of whale and for porpoises to be sent up to the
royal kitchen show that they were more than
tolerated. Not, of course, that they could for a

moment be classed with such a dainty as the lamprey, which proved fatal to the first Henry. " Lamprey fresshe baken " figured in the feast of Henry V, and a contemporary cookery-book gives elaborate instructions for the preparation of such a dish, of which the most curious part refers to the raising of the crust : " Skald the Lampray and pare him clene and couche hym round on the cofyn tyl he be helyd [covered] ; then kyvere hym fayre with a lid save a lytel hole in the myddelle, and at that hool blow in the cofynne with thine mowthe a gode blast of wynde, and sodenly stoppe the hole, that the wynd abyde withynne to reyse uppe the cofynne that he falle not adowne ; and whan he is a lytel y-hardid in the oven pryke the cofyn with a pynne y-steked on a roddys ende, for brekyng of the cofynne, and than lat bake and serve forth colde." If this method of raising the crust is still practised in the kitchen one would prefer to remain in ignorance of the fact. As there was a proper manner of preparing lamprey pie, so there was a proper manner of serving it when it came to table, —as anyone familiar with the elaborate science of carving as practised in the Middle Ages might guess :

" Fresshe lamprey bake, thus it must be dight :
  Open the pastey lid, therin to have a sight,
  Take then white bred, thyn y-kut and light,
  Lay it in a chargere, dische or platter right ;
  With a spone then take owt the gentille galantyne,
  In the dische on the bred lay hit, lemman myne,
  Then take powder of Synamome and temper hit
    with red wyne,—
  The same wold plese a pore man, y suppose, well
    and fyne ;—

Medieval Cookery

Mynse ye the gobyns as thyn as a grote
Then lay them uppon youre galantyne stondinge on .
    a chaffire hoote."

Although it might be difficult for the inexperienced to perform correctly the ceremony of carving
a lamprey pie, with its elaborate ritual of heating
up the gravy on a chafing-dish and so forth, it
would at any rate be easier to get some result than
in the case of the crustaceans, for " crabbe is a
slutte to kerve and a wrawd wight," and lobster
is little better. Even the miniature shrimp is
more bother than he is worth, and the best thing
that one old writer can say of them is that they
" give a kind of exercise for such as be weak ; for
head and brest must first be divided from their
bodies ; then each of them must be dis-scaled and
clean picked with much pidling." Still, shrimps
were occasionally eaten for supper by the monks
of Winchester, who were also addicted to oysters
by way of entrée, though the oyster as a rule does
not seem to have been in demand,—I cannot trace
it on the menu of any banquet, and it appears to
have ranked little higher than the humble " mus-
cule " in public estimation. On the other hand,
much more importance was attached to the various
kinds of fresh-water fish which we for the last three
generations have treated with increasing neglect.
Trout, of course, are too delicious ever to fall out
of fashion, and eels still command a certain market,
though not used in the vast quantities once customary, but who that is not himself a fisherman
ever eats the once admired pike and carp ? Still
less appreciated are the barbel, perch, tench,
bream, gudgeon, and roach, all once thought

worthy to appear at a king's table. Therein, perhaps, we show wisdom, for " fysshes of the see, the which have skales or many fynnes, be more holsomer than the fresshe-water fysshe," and also better flavoured. The latter is all the more important since the decay of cookery has laid us open to the charge of having many religions but only one fish-sauce, whereas the converse was the case with our ancestors, who were skilled in sauces and could even make an appetising dish out of such unpromising material as the much-dried stockfish, as one of them bears witness ; " I have eaten of a pie made onely with stockefishe whiche hath been verie good, but the goodnesse was not so much in the fishe as in the cookerie, which may make that savorie which of itself is unsavorie." The stock-fish was the finny counterpart of " Martilmas beef," that is to say, beef killed about Martinmas (November 11th) and cured by hanging in the smoke. Such hanged beef Andrew Borde considered more useful as a waterproof than as a food, for " if a man have a pece hangynge by his syde and another in his bely, that the whiche doth hange by the syde shall do hym more good yf a showre of rayne do chaunse than that the which is in his bely." In other words, it was for external application only, in which it differed from " charde-quynce," or quince marmalade, which " is comfortable for a mannys body, and namely for the Stomak." By the way, I wonder how many people realise that marmalade is essentially and derivatively a preserve of quinces, and that its application to " orenges in succade " is comparatively recent. So also is its use as a breakfast dish. Breakfast was formerly a meal to which little importance was attached and of which we therefore hear little, though in the days of the British Solomon one writer laid it down that " he that eateth everie day tender Onions with Honey to his breakfast shall live the more healthfull."

The opinion just quoted on the value of onions might be supported by one given eighty years earlier that " onyons maketh a mans appetyde good and putteth away fastydyousnes." On the other hand, a writer intermediate between these two considered that onions injured the memory, " because they annoy the Eyes with dazeling dimnesse through a hoate vapour," while a much later author summed up the more obvious peculiarities of that pungent root in his declaration that " onions make a man stink and wink." There appears to be an idea rather prevalent that in the Middle Ages there were very few vegetables, and only a little while ago I saw it stated definitely that cabbages had not been introduced into England much more than a hundred years, whereas they occur in the fifteenth-century cookery books, and the " pot herbs " of which the tithes were payable to the vicar of Henfield were defined in 1409 as " cabbages and leeks and other herbs of which broth is made by the custom of the country." Some idea of the variety of the " other herbs " may be gathered from a contemporary recipe for pottage, which begins : " Take Borage, Vyolet, Malwys, Percely, Yong Wortys, Bete, Avence, Longebeff (a kind of bugloss), with Orage and other." Several of these herbs have fallen into disuse ; borage lingers in our claret cup, and mallows, avens, and " longebeff " may be left unregretted in oblivion, but the loss of violets is sad, especially as " Almon-butter made with fyne suger and good rose-water and eaten with the flowers of many vyolettes is a commendable dysshe, specyallye in Lent, whan the vyoletes be fragrant ; it rejoyseth the herte, it doth comforte the brayne, and doth qualyfye the heate of the lyver." There was also in the fifteenth century a dish called " Vyolette," made of almond milk and rice flour flavoured with " Gyngere, Galyngale, Pepir, Datys, Fygys, and Rasonys y-corven," and coloured with saffron, " and when thou dressyste, take the flowres and hew them and styre it therwith ; nym the braunchys with the flowres and sette above and serve it forth." Similar pleasant compounds were made with red roses, primroses, and hawthorn flowers, and the variety of herbs and plants called in aid would imply that the average cook believed that " there is no Herbe nor weede but God hath gyven vertue to them to helpe man." At the same time there was no tendency to vegetarianism, and, however deeply versed in herb-lore, the medieval cook might exclaim with him in Plautus :

> " Like other cooks I do not supper dress
>   That put whole medows in a platter,
> And make no better of the guests than beeves
>   With herbs and grass to feed them fatter."

Vegetables are all very well in their way, but most men of those days would have agreed with Nebuchadnezzar what time he " champed the unwonted food," that " it may be wholesome but it is not good."

Medieval Cookery

" Their lives that eat such food must needs be short ;
And 'tis a fearful thing for to report,
That men should feed on such a kind of meat
Which very juments would refuse to eat."

Space fails me to dilate upon pheasant eaten
with sugar and mustard, upon " grete pyes " each
containing the whole stock of a poulterer's shop,
or upon the varieties and virtues, or otherwise, of
meats. But few will disagree with the statement
that " the flessh of an olde ramme wyll not lightely
disgest, and that is very evyll," or the similar
axiom of another sage that " olde beefe and kowe
flesshe doth ingender melancolye." Banquets
began and ended with fruits, and the servant was
instructed before retiring to ascertain whether his
master would have " any conceites after dinner as
appels, nuts, or creame," or such fruits as straw-
berries, which " be praysed above all buryes, for
they dothe ingender good blode, eaten with suger."
At the same time " Rawe crayme undecocted,
eaten with strawberyes or hurtes, is a rurall
mannes banket. I have knowen such bankettes
hath putt men in jeoperdy of theyr lyves " ; wherefore " Be ware of cowe creme and of good strawberyes, hurtelberyes, jouncat, for these wyll make
your soverayne seke but he ete harde chese."

VI. Medieval Medicine ✍ ✍ ✍

"LORDES, Ladies and Gentylmen, learned
and unlerned, of what estate or degree so
ever you be of, thynke not that no man can be
holpen by no maner of medecynes if so be God do
sende the sicknes ; for he hath put a tyme to every
man, over the which tyme no man by no art nor
science can not prolonge the time. But this
aforesayde tyme a man may shorten or abreviate
many wayes, concerning that God hath geven man
in this lyfe free wyl. Nowe we havyng this free
wyll dyvers tymes do kyll our bodyes as much as
lyeth in us : . . . but God, knowynge at the
begynnying of the creacion of the worlde that man
wolde be prone many wayse to abreviate his lyfe,
made then provision that man myght be holpen,
by his grace and the vertue whiche he dyd gyve to
herbes, wedes, trees, rootes, fruites and stones.
The propertie and vertue of the whiche, fewe men
or none doth knowe them except doctours of
phisicke and such as doth labour to have the
knowledge of theyr operacions."

Such we may take to be the official attitude of
the medical faculty, the justification for the
existence of a separate class of medicine men.
They are the interpreters to the unlearned of the
healing secrets of God, or of Nature, if you prefer
to substitute that vague unknown goddess for the
very personal deity in whom our forbears embodied
their conception of the First Cause. It must,

however, be admitted that the laity have at times
held other views as to the position occupied by
doctors in actual fact, as opposed to theory and
have not hesitated to express those views. The
Dutch proverb that " a new physician must have
a new churchyard," and the unkind suggestion
that the old doctor, buried in the cemetery of the
village where he had so long practised, should take
the epitaph of Sir Christopher Wren—*Si monumen-
tum requiris, circumspice*—are but the echoes of
gibes that were ancient in the days of Pliny, and
had lost their freshness when medical science was
first reduced to order by

> " Ypocras the goode surgean
> And Socrates and Galean
> That were filosophers alle thre
> That tyme the best in any cuntre."

As Petrarch, with whom detestation of doctors
was almost a religion, shuddered to hear that Pope
Clement in his sickness was surrounded by
physicians, so in 1464 Margaret Paston wrote
anxiously to her husband : " For Goddys sake be
war what medecyne ye take of any fysissyans of
London ; I schal never trust to hem, because of
your fader and myn onkyl, whoys sowlys God
assoyle."

So Piers the Ploughman learnt the " lovely
lessoun " that " morthereres are mony leches,
lorde hem amende ! Thei do men dye thorw ther
drynkes ere destine it wolde." So the anti-
clerical satirist of the early fourteenth century
railed against the " false fisiciens that helpen men
to die," and so a hundred and fifty years earlier

the common people said that physicians were " the class of men who kill other men in the most polite and courteous way."

Not that it must be supposed, from my quoting these unkind reflections, that I myself am one of Geyler's thirteenth battalion of fools—those who despise medicine and make a mock of doctors. Rather I would cry with John of Salisbury : " God forbid that I should say anything bad about them ! They should rather be soothed by politeness than angered by words, and I do not wish that they should treat me hardly when, for my sins, I fall into their hands." At the same time it must be admitted that, whatever may be the case now, the leech in medieval times was not always as learned and well grounded as that " verrey parfit prac- tisour " who beguiled the way to Canterbury with the touching and moral tale of Appius Claudius and Virginia. There was many a leech who had but a hazy knowledge of

> " the olde Esculapius,
> And Deiscorides and eek Rufus,
> Old Hypocras, Haly and Galien
> Serapyon, Razis and Avicen,
> Averrois, Damascen and Constantyn,
> Bernard and Gatesden and Gilbertyn,"

and yet ventured to practise, to make a show of learning, and to administer fearsome empirical compounds. To excuse his blunder if the patient die, or to emphasise his skill if, by reason of a strong constitution, he survive both the disease and the remedy, such a physician first exaggerates the danger of the case,

Medieval Medicine

" And swereth that he is sekere than ever yit he was,
   and sein,
 Dame, for faute of helpe thine housebonde is neir
   slein."

Then, with equally impressive manner, he vows to
save the sick man, " thouh he wit no more than a
goos whether he will live or die." Whatever the
outcome of his treatment, the doctor would see to
it that he got his fee ; and if he were wise, he would
secure part at any rate of it before beginning his
attendance, or at all events before completing it,
for *Mox fugit a mente medicus morbo recedente.*
This maxim, as " somme understonden Englysch
that kan nouther Latyn nor Frensch," we may
render freely by an adaptation of a well-known
couplet :

" The Devil was sick, the Devil would pay a fee ;
  The Devil got well, the devil a fee paid he."

It was impressed frequently enough upon those
unbusiness-like or too confiding doctors, who relied
upon their patients' gratitude for their reward.
Take the case, for instance, of Philip Barrowe, an
Elizabethan practitioner, who, when William
Adams, a Cambridgeshire draper, was grievously
afflicted with " a most infectious and hated
disease," the exact nature of which is left in
merciful obscurity, spent five or six weeks in constant attendance on him, and " nothinge respected
his owne waightie affayres in comparison of the
other's health." For this he considered that he
ought to have been offered at least £20, but
apparently he did not like to ask, and the patient

was as silent as the Tar Baby. Not to be sent away quite empty-handed, Philip helped himself to some broad-cloth and satin from his patient's shop, and then the ungrateful wretch " contrary to humanity " sued him for the value of the goods. Such cases were not uncommon, but another that occurred about the same time suggests that occasionally the position was reversed. John Burye, esquire, called in Thomas Hawle of Oxford, " then beinge but a yonge student and not knowen or reputed but for a surgyon," to treat his leg, which " casually by reason of a falle from a horse was brooken in sonder in the thyghe." Hawle " bothe mistooke the place wheare the boune was broken and also made incysyons in the legge contrary to alle arte and knowledge," with the result that John Burye, after being " paynefullye tormented by the space of seven months," died. Then Hawle, who had already been paid much more than he deserved, had the impudence to claim fees at the rate of 10s. a day, although he had said that as he was only a surgeon his fee would be 3s. 4d. From this we may learn not to employ young and inexperienced medical men, but to " Be ware of that leech which by thee woulde take experyens howe he myght hele another." And, as an erstwhile medical student of Cambridge, I feel I am also entitled to point out that it was the Oxford student who bungled his case, and the Cambridge patient who was ungrateful.

In the two instances last quoted it must be borne in mind that we have heard only one side, but in a case which occurred in the time of " King Harry the viij of most worthy memory," we have the versions of Peter Starkey, draper, of London, and

of Baltazar de Gracyes, or de Quarcyes, surgeon.
According to the draper, one Alexander Martyn,
servant to the Bishop of London, was afflicted
with an unpleasant disease ; Baltazar was called
in and agreed to cure him. For this he was to have
five marks (£3 6s. 8d.) down, another five marks
" when yt shuld be knowen and percevyd by
mans reason " that he was cured, and a further
five marks if after a year the disease had not
reappeared ; for the payment of which Peter
Starkey made himself responsible. Alexander,
however, was not cured, and the Bishop had
to get another servant ; but as soon as the Bishop
was dead, Baltazar came down upon the miserable
Starkey and demanded payment. On the other
hand, the surgeon complained that he had " healed
hym of all deseasis infirmytes and sekenessis
which he had within hys body," except that he
" leffte a littell issue to be rynnyng in oon of his
lyggys for preservacion of his lyff "—as a sort of
safety-valve, in fact—but that, instead of paying
the remainder of the £10 due, Alexander had sued
him for the five marks paid in advance.

The Bishop of London ought to have been able
to select a good surgeon for his servant, as he had
the licensing of medical men for the city. How
early he exercised this power I do not know, but
during the sixteenth century the duly licensed
members of the profession showed increasing
jealousy of unqualified practitioners, and actions
were constantly brought against offenders. In
1524 we find Dr. Bentley and Dr. Yakesley, complaining that Roger Smith, " appotecari," Roys
at the Grey Friars, and Westcott, were practising
physic, " havying no maner speculation and

cunnyng that to doo." Of these particular offenders, Roger " Smyth " is mentioned in the accounts of the Earl of Rutland for 1533 as being paid £7 13s. 4d. " for his payne takyn with my Lord in his fevir," and a further 32s. 10d. " for such stuff as he spent about my Lord in the tyme of his sekenesse." The name is, I fear, too common to allow us to connect him with a contemporary Richard Smythe, " doctor of physyke," who, being licensed by the University at Cambridge, incurred the jealousy of " Doctor Buttes, Physichen, then ther inhabitynge." That worthy, who was doctor to Henry VIII, and was immortalised by Holbein's pencil, went so far as to get hold of his rival's licence and cut off the seal. However, the University, " of ther charitable myndes and frewyll " sealed fresh letters for him and he then went to the University of Louvain for four years. Returning to London, he was duly admitted by Bishop Cuthbert Tunstall in the presence of four medical men, but in spite of this Martin Pery and Anthony Lowe, " persons which leyve by pollynge and scharynge " brought actions against him as unqualified. Nor was this his only misfortune ; for after he had cured one William Wotton the ungrateful man caused a friend with the appropriate name of William Lyar to entice Richard Smythe to the Tower on pretence of a patient requiring his aid ; on his arrival he was arrested at Wotton's suit and two persons assaulted him, one of whom, drawing a dagger, would have slain him " if he had not wislie with spede escaped frome them." Professional jealousy, again, was responsible for the actions brought against Robert Jackson, who dared, according to his own account, to cure without licence patients whom the properly qualified practitioners could not or would not cure. It seems that one Henry Wellys, being diseased with " sondry and grevous sorys and malidies " resorted to Danby and Vicars, two of the leading Tudor surgeons. How they treated his body does not appear, except that they did more harm than good, but they bled his purse to the uttermost, and afterwards " wolde no more mynester medisens to hym by reason of his poverte." Robert Jackson then took pity on him, and healed his infirmities without aggravating his poverty ; he also cured gratuitously " a pore man called John Crowe, beying in grete jeperdie of deth by reason of bledyng." The chief result of his kindness was that he was threatened with heavy penalties, although he protested that he had not practised in London and had taken no money for his services.

Some fifty years later than the case last quoted there was a pretty quarrel between Edward Sculles of Newington, a specialist in the cure of fistula, and Edward Owen, surgeon. Owen, who had been a haberdasher before he adopted the more learned profession, had been treating a child, John Bowyer of Kingston, for fistula, with such small success that at last he brought him up to Surgeons' Hall for a consultation. There the majority of the surgeons decided that the boy must be suffering from some internal disease as well, but Sculles declined to accept this verdict, and although the surgeons " tooke the same in greefe," proved his case by curing the sufferer, whereby he incurred the enmity of the ex-haberdasher. Sculles had an eminent predecessor in John of Arderne ; who

began to specialise in the treatment of fistula
about the date of the Black Death, and wrought
many remarkable cures, " of which the first was
Sir Adam Everyngham of Laxton in the Clay byside
Tukkesford, whiche Sir Adam for sothe was in
Gascone with Sir Henry, that tyme named herle
of Derby and afterwards was made Duke of Lan-
castre, a noble and worthy lord." Sir Adam
" made for to aske counsell at all the lechez and
corurgienz that he myghte fynd in Gascone, in
Burdeux, at Briggerac, Tolows and Neyybon and
Peyters and many other places, and all forsoke
hym for uncurable ; whiche y-se and y-herde, the
forsaid Adam hastied for to torne home to his
contree, and when he come home he did off al his
knyghtly clothings and cladde mournyng clothes
in purpose of abydyng dissolvyng or lesyng of his
body beyng nygh to hym." Fortunately Arderne
took him in hand and cured him so completely
that he " ledde a glad life 30 yere and more," his
physician gaining thereby much renown. Afterwards he cured " Hugon Derlyng of Fowick of
Balne by Snaythe, Johan Schefed of Rightwell
aside Tekill, and Sir Raynald Grey, lord of Wilton
in Wales and lord of Schirlond byside Chesterfelde,
whiche asked consel at the moste famose lechez of
Ynglond and none availed hym," as well as many
others of less resonant title. From the consideration of fistula our minds turn naturally to a
disease occasionally confused with it—scrofula or
" the King's evil." It is not unnatural that the
men of the Middle Ages, with their beliefs in miracle
of healing and in the divinity that doth hedge a
king, should have attributed healing powers to
the royal touch, but why this particular disease

should have been considered susceptible to kingly influence is not obvious. For the matter of that, it is equally difficult to see why the top joint of the second finger of the right hand should be dedicated to St. Simon Cleophas, while the second joint of the third finger of the left hand is under the protection of St. Bartholomew. The appropriation of diseases to saints presents many puzzles, at least to those who have not the *Acta Sanctorum* at their finger-tips or stored in formidable array upon their shelves. What, for instance, has St. Blaise to do with the quinsey, St. Herbert with hydrophobia, or St. Martin with the itch? On the other hand, it is obvious that fellow-feeling made St. Roche patron of plague—who, judging from his unmannerly insistence upon the display of his diseased leg from the walls of every picture gallery in Italy, must have been a member of the district-visited class—and St. Nicaise patron of small-pox; for, as the poet puts it, with a nice derangement of pronouns,

> " Seint Nicasse had a pokke small
> And mekyll grevans he hadde wyth all,
> He preyed to God that hym dere boughte
> That qwo so indyrly hym besoughte
> That he hym from the pockys schuld ware
> Gif he on hym hys name writ bare."

So also with St. Apollonia. Having suffered martyrdom at the hands of wild dentists, she naturally took charge of the teeth, and in a sixteenth century manuscript on my shelves her portrait appears, carrying a formidable pair of pincers, at the head of a supplication for preserva-

tion from diseases of the teeth. But at least one
early sufferer from toothache seems to have felt
that a single saint, and she a woman, afforded
insufficient protection against that dire evil, and
accordingly evolved a much more potent charm for
" the tethe-werke," which he apparently attributed
to the malefic influence of a loathly worm :

> " I conjure thee, laythely beeste, with that ilke spere
> That Longyons in his hand gane bare,
> And also with ane hatte of thorne
> That on my Lordis hede was borne,
> With alle the wordis mare and lesse,
> With the Office of the Messe,
> With my Lorde and his xii postilles,
> With oure Ladye and her x maydenys,
> Saynt Margrete the haly quene,
> Saynt Katerin the haly virgyne,
> ix tymes Goddis forbott, thou wikkyde worme,
> Thet ever thou make any restynge,
> Bot awaye mot thou wende
> To the erthe and the stane."

Whatever the reason may have been, to return
from our digression, the fact remains that the
English kings, from Edward the Confessor onwards,
for six centuries and a half, exercised the practice
of touching scrofulous cases, and the evidence for
recovery following such touching is too strong to
be rejected, however it may be explained. Henry
II is recorded to have wrought such cures.
Edward I, during a tour through the southern
counties in 1278, touched an enormous number of
patients, batches of two and three hundred being
treated in a single week. Each person touched
received at this time a penny—the only denomina-

Medieval Medicine

tion of coinage then in circulation—and under later monarchs a gold piece, the king's evil being the only disease for the healing of which the physician paid a fee. Henry VII seems to have instituted a regular religious ceremonial for use on these occasions, and his son probably took a scientific interest in the disease. For Henry VIII dabbled in physic as he did in music and many other arts, and wrote quite a number of prescriptions. His tastes in this, as in other matters, tended to be florid, and his medicines are chiefly notable for lavishness of ingredients. " A plastre devised by the Kinges Majestie at Grenewich and made at Westminster " contained leaves of plantain, violet, honeysuckle, and comfrey, and rosebuds, boiled up with " fatte of capons or hennys," to which was added litharge of silver, red coral, hartshorn, unicorn's (*i.e.* narwhal's) horn and pearls, the resultant mixture being made up with a mucilage of linseed, " quynsede " and other things to make a " spasmadrappe " or plaster. " The Kinges Maiestie's owne plastre " contained many similar ingredients, including coral and gold and silver, substances which medieval physicians put into the medicine of their wealthier patients chiefly as a homeopathic device, to draw more gold and silver into their own pockets. It was, however, an age of prodigious compounds,—" 300 simples in a julip, potion or a little pill." Such a popular patent medicine as the " Drynke of Anteoche " contained a full score of different herbs—bugle, comfrey, briar, hemp, tansy, red nettle, " Osmound," pimpernel, " orpyn," mouse-ear, avence, betony, herb Walter and herb Robert—boiled with white wine and honey for " the space of this psalme, seying *Miserere mei deus.*" It would be easy but tiresome to fill pages with similar and even more elaborate compounds, each a miniature herbarium in itself, but one is tempted to sweep them aside with the comment of the learned Fuchsius of Nuremburg : " Many an old wife or country woman doth often more good with a few known and common garden herbs than our bumbast physicians with all their prodigious, sumptuous, far fetched, rare, conjecturall medicines."

" Drynke of Anteoche " had at least the advantage of being purely herbal, while many of the mixtures, especially the " electuaries," combined the elements of the three kingdoms. Of minerals, we have already referred to gold and silver and coral. Pounded precious stones, and pearls in particular, figured in the medieval pharmacopœia, and their merits in a whole and uncompounded state were also recognised, it being considered a wise precaution to " hold sometimes in your mouth either a Hyacinth [*i.e.* a jacinth] or a Crystall or a Granat, or pure Gold or Silver, or else sometimes pure Sugarcandy." Ivory, also, was a fairly common ingredient. It occurs in two fourteenth-century prescriptions for jaundice ; in the first, the patient is to be washed three times with water containing wormwood and than " gyf hym to drynk yvore schavyn smal in wyne." In the other ivory and saffron are to be mixed with holy water and drunk in the morning and at night " when thu gas to bedde." It might also be said to have been recommended for external application, if we consider the advice to " combe your head softly and easily with an ivorie combe, for nothing recreateth the memorie more," but here

Medieval Medicine

I fear the merit lay in the comb rather than in the material. Turning to the vegetable kingdom we find ourselves overwhelmed with an innumerable multitude of herbs and plants, fruits and roots, from the humble daisy of the English countryside to " sena, cassia out of Ægypt, rubarbe from Barbarye, aloes from Zocotora, turbith, agarick, mirabolanes, hermodactils from the East Indies." Every plant that grew had its medicinal qualities, and some were so full of merit that they were good for almost all the ills to which the flesh is heir. Betony was one of these cure-alls, a proof of its virtue being that if that deaf but wise serpent, the adder, receives any injury, it crawls on to a plant of betony and is cured. This makes it the more curious that the same writer who asserts this on the authority of his own experience (" That have I seyn with eye in gaderynge of betonye ") should go on to say :

> " Who so wyll don a serpent tene,
> Make a garland of betonye grene,
> And make a circle hym rownde abowte ;
> And he schall never on lyve go owte
> But with hys tayle he schall hym schende
> Or with his mowth hym self to rende."

So far as the purely medicinal qualities of betony are concerned, it may be mentioned that a nerve tonic can be made of

> " iiij levys of betonye fyne
> And iij cupful of elde wyne
> And greynes of pepir xx and vij
> Alle togedere groundyn even."

More Medieval Byways

If, however, this tonic proves insufficient to brace up the patient's nerves, and he becomes subject to what modern physicians call hallucinations but our ancestors called evil spirits, then this same invaluable plant affords him a remedy, for

> " Who so betonye on hym bare
> Fro wykked sperytes it wyll hym ware ;
> In the monyth of August on all wyse
> It muste be gaderyd ere sonne ryse."

In the same way rosemary, betony's closest rival in multiplicity of virtues, is " contrarious to develys and to wikkyd spirtys as the stone is that is called jet " ; it was also a protection against thunder and lightning, wherein it surpassed the laurel, which was efficacious against thunder but not against lightning. The powder of rosemary caused its user to be " graciowse and i-loved in al sight," but was inferior to henbane, which if carried on a man's person shall make all women love him. Henbane was another of the herbs obnoxious to spirits, as " nygromanseris " well knew, and resembled St. John's wort in repelling " suche malyfycyousnes or spirites." Medicinally, henbane could be used to prepare an oil " wonderfully gude to the goute." For this purpose the leaves must be gathered on Midsummer Eve, and put into a pot with holes in the bottom ; the pot, with a vessel underneath to catch the distillation, is then to be buried under the hearthstone, on which the fire is to be made during the following twelve months, at the end of which time it is to be dug up, when the healing oil will be found in the lower vessel.

Medieval Medicine

To obtain the full virtues of any herb, it was often essential to gather it under a certain aspect of the moon or planets and frequently with the muttered accompaniment of charms or prayers. Thus, for the cure of "web in the eye," it was essential that the red honeysuckle, whose juice was to be commingled with marrow from "ye grete bone of ye gosys winge," should be gathered with the saying of nine paternosters, nine aves and a creed. For this same disease, or its variation known as "pin and web" an amazingly horrid cure can be found by the curious in "The Countess of Kent's Choice Manual." Andrew Borde gives the alternatives of an operation or the injection of the juice of horehound or licorice, and it was probably the latter treatment that was employed, in the last decade of the fifteenth century, by Peter Blank, surgeon, who undertook to cure the son of Simon Lynd, stationer, of London, who was "diseased in the ie with a pynne and a wabbe." Blank, however, stipulated that the child should be "preserved and kepte from mysbehavyng hymself with his hands in toching and robbyng of the seyd ie," and, as this condition, was not observed, disclaimed all responsibility for his failure to effect a cure.

Having touched on the mineral and vegetable substances used in early medicine, we may give a little consideration to animal substances. Why the smell of a fox should be good for palsy I do not know, but Andrew Borde asserts that such is the case, and advises that the patient suffering from that disease should be bathed with water in which the cut up carcase of a fox has been soaked with "calamynt and balme and carawayes." Some two

centuries before Borde's time, an approved remedy
for quinsy consisted chiefly of the dripping from a
stuffed and roasted cat—stuffed in the culinary and
not in the taxidermic sense. The recipe or pre-
scription is perhaps worth giving in full : " For
hym that haves the squinansy : tak a fatte katte
and fla hit wale, and clene, and draw oute the
guttes, and tak the grees of an urcheon [*i.e.* a
hedgehog] and the fatte of a bare, and resynes and
einy greke and sauge and gumme of wodebynde
and virgyn wax : al this mye smal, and forse the
catte within als thu forses a goos, rost hit hale
and gader the grees and enoynt hym tharwith."
Those, however, who do not feel inclined to try
this cure can take refuge in the favourite medieval
practice of phlebotomy, provided they know which
vein to open :—" It is gude for to blede on the
tonge for the squnesy." This seems reasonable,
nor is there anything surprising in the fact, or at
least statement, that " Under the nose, on the ende
therof, lygges a vayn that is gud to opyne for the
fransy in the hed " ; it has, indeed, often been
noticed that the drawing of blood from the nose,
even with such a simple instrument as the knuckles,
has a sobering effect upon the frenzied ; but it is
a mystery why " the vayne betwyx the fyngere
and the thombe is gud to be opyd for migrams
in the hed." Returning to our animals, but
omitting the more nauseous remedies, we may
remark that in many cases a good deal of
cruelty was involved through the use of live
creatures. For jaundice a live tench was to be
taken, but, as it was to be cut in half and
boned, it must have been dead before it was applied
to the patient's ribs. For gout, young ravens

were to be taken alive out of their nest, " and loke
that thei touche not the erthe nor that thei comyn
in non hows," and to be burnt to powder in a new
pot, and, as a charm to produce fever, a fourteenth
century writer prescribes a live adder and nine
" horned wormys that man calles the nutres
[newtes] " to be boiled alive and the victim's
hands, feet and " thunwanges " (the pleasing
Saxon word for the temples) to be anointed with
the resultant grease. Worms, of the hornless
variety, were neither the most uncommon nor the
most unpleasant ingredient in old prescriptions,
and " pouldre of long wormes well washed and
dryed " formed part of " a cataplasme made
unguentlyke " by the device of Henry VIII, while
a century earlier one treatment for dropsy—" a
sekeness full mervelyous and to yonge And elde full
perylous "—was to

> " Take grete erthe wormes thryis thre
> That all the hedys smit off be,
> And in holy watyr tempere hem smal,
> And sukyr or lycoryce menge with all,
> That the dropyk drynke ix wormyss ilke day,
> Lessand the nombres of the wormys ay
> Tyll ix dayes be comyn and goon ;
> Thow hym thynkyth it shulde hym sloon."

The wording of these directions is a little obscure,
but apparently the patient, whose objection to
the remedy is foretold in the last line, was to take
nine worms the first day, eight the next, and so on
until the ninth day, when he would be quit alike of
worms and dropsy. After all, there is really little
more to object to in a diet of worms than in a dish
of snails, and Frenchmen have assured me that the
latter are excellent, though I have never yet

ventured to test their accuracy, and still prefer to eat my snails at secondhand as in " A Medicine to restore Nature in a Man :—Take iij chekynes or iiij as ye like, and put them in a coope to feed as I shall teche you. Fyrste take a quantyte of whete and put yt in clene watyr, and then gadyr a good quantyte of snayles that bear howses on them," (as opposed to the houseless slugs or " red snayles, that crepyn abowte in reyn and haylys ") " and put them thereto as they be shelles and all ; and so thanne boyle all these togyder, the whete and the snaylles in water. Then take out the whete by hymselfe and the watyr by hymselfe and caste away the shelles and the corruptyon of the snaylles. And with that whete fede the checons and with brede amonge, and let them drynke of the watyr and of none other watyr. And when ye be dysposyd ete a chekyn one day, rostyd, and ij dayes after another and so contynue as ye fynd yt doth you good."

But we are wandering dangerously far afield, for though diet is a branch, or even the main stem, of physic, if we once stray into that fruitful field and start discussing the relative wholesomeness of mutton and veal and the dishes appropriate to the varying temperaments and constitutions, there is no knowing where, or when, we shall reach an end. But I cannot refrain from quoting the Edwardian rhymester's feeling complaint against the " false fisicien " :

" He doth the wif sethe a capoun and a piece beef,
 Ne gif the gode man noht therof, be him never so lief;
 The best he piketh up himself and maketh his mawe
  touht ;
 And geveth the gode man soupe, the lene broth that
  his nought."

VII. Tinimies[1]

" Fro Venyse to Port Jaff by the see
  Hyt ys two thowsand myle and hundrys thre ;
  And yn that see there ys a place
  Wher the whale swalowyd Jonas."

AND there were a good many other queer
things in the sea at that time, if we may
accept the accounts of contemporary travellers
who had listened to the enchanting strains of mer-
maids or witnessed with terror strange, half-human
forms climb up the sides of their ship and, sitting
on its prow, threaten to submerge it in the swirling
waves. As to great sea serpents, far be it from
me to include them in the same category with the
sea bishops, sea elephants and sea unicorns with
which the writers of bestiaries—it would hardly be
correct to call them works on natural history—
exercised their imaginations and edified their
readers. It is legitimate to scoff at the many-eyed
sea sow of Aldrovandus,—not, by the way, to be
confounded with the real sea pig, the " porkpisce "
or porpoise—but in the face of so much evidence
both ancient and modern it would be rash to deny
the existence of a sea serpent, who would be quite
capable of confuting scepticism by turning up
unexpectedly in mid-Atlantic, or even off the

[1] Is there any unfortunate reader that does not know the
story of the little girl who, when she first saw the sea, asked,
" But where are the Tinimies ? "—justifying her expectancy on
the grounds that " In six days the Lord made heaven and earth,
the sea and all the tinimies."

Brighton pier. It is the African capacity of the sea for producing something new that lends its chief charm to sea-fishing, and there is a similar excitement about a pursuit which is usually considered much drier, record searching. It is one of the most pleasing and exasperating features of that pursuit that one is always liable to stumble suddenly upon some unexpected piece of information in some improbable place. And while it is pleasant enough to have difficulties solved and puzzles explained by such a lucky discovery it is peculiarly exasperating that such a find is usually made too late or, which is even worse, too early, for in the latter case one is left with a vague and indefinite recollection of having once seen in some unlikely spot the very record which would afford the missing clue. It so happens that a little while back I was working, for my own purposes on records dealing with the tackle and other constituent parts of medieval ships. Having finished with the subject and laid it aside, I landed by chance upon an excellent contemporary description of the sort of horizontal capstan, used in the thirteenth century for hoisting the great sail or, upon occasion, weighing anchor. The account occurred in a catalogue of miracles of St. Thomas of Canterbury, and related how Gerard of Dover, having dropped his anchor, wished to raise it again. First of all two sailors went forward, as usual in such cases, and standing on the prow drew on the rope, but the flukes had caught in something immovable, and although the whole crew came and hauled the anchor remained fixed. " Wherefore, turning to their last resource, they put the end of the cable round the beam, which

the sailors call ' the windas.' Now this is a beam
placed right across the poop, and having holes in
its sides, and it is used in the bigger ships for
hoisting the sail. For spokes, or bars, are inserted
into the holes, and what unaided strength cannot
effect can be done by the leverage of the bars, for
as the beam, with the ropes wrapped round it,
is turned round, the task, by means of the beam,
is made easy." In this particular case, however,
even the " windas " proved ineffectual until one
of the mariners had the brilliant inspiration to call
upon St. Thomas for help, when, of course, the
anchor rose like a trout to a fly. St. Thomas, who
in his lifetime had been driven back by adverse
winds when he first attempted to escape from
England, after his death was constantly able and
willing to control the elements for the benefit of his
devotees. He would save an Irish ship from the
wreckers of the west coast, float a derelict off the
sands and send it merrily in pursuit of its crew
and bring vessels out of the most perilous
storms safe to shore, or if necessary, do the converse, as in the case of the Danish merchant, who
built a ship so huge that when the King of Den-
mark came to Sleswick to see it launched it stuck
fast and was only saved by the intervention of the
English saint from the ignominious fate of having
to be broken up.

It is curious that St. Nicholas should have been
the patron of sailors rather than the fisherman St.
Peter, but the latter seems to have had a certain
vogue, especially on the Yorkshire coast. The
fishermen of Redcar used to hold a feast on St.
Peter's Day, and at Whitby it was customary
" yerely on midsomer even Seynt Peter even and

Seynt Thomas even, at the tyme of the bonefyers accustomed to be made in the honour of God of tyme oute of man's remembraunce," for all the shipmasters and mariners, "accompanied with other yong peple" to have carried before them blazing tar barrel on a staff "and the maryners to followe too and too, and to syng throught the strettes and to resorte to every bonefier and ther to drynke and make mery with songes and other honeste pastyme." On one occasion, just before the Dissolution of the Monasteries, the servants of the Abbot of Whitby interfered with the procession, throwing stones as it came up a steep and narrow street. The natural result was a scuffle, for seafaring men are not a mild-mannered race ; in fact, a suffragan was once appointed to assist a bishop of Chichester expressly on the grounds that his diocese was inhabited largely by sailors who were notoriously quarrelsome, so that churchyards were constantly being polluted by bloodshed and requiring reconsecration. These same Sussex seamen, or at least such of them as came from the Cinque Ports in the eastern part of the county, gave proof of their pugnacity in the " Herring War." This struggle of the Kent and Sussex ports with Yarmouth culminated in August, 1297, when the rival fleets were lying at Sluys after transporting the English troops. A chance brawl in a tavern was the spark which kindled the conflagration, and a battle royal ensued in which the Portsmen burnt sixteen of the eastern ships, including several of the biggest, such as the *Sainte Croyz* of the exceptional size of 240 tons, the *Grenewolde* and two *Swans*, all of about 150 tons, and slew two hundred men of their crews. The mildness with which King

Edward treated this outbreak, suggests that still, as thirty years earlier, when they sided with Simon de Montfort against King Henry, "the sayd wardeyns of v portes had the domynyon of the see, wherefore the Kynge was fayne to folowe their pleasures." But it must not be supposed that the bloodshed and violence was all on one side; things were pretty evenly balanced, and even allowing for their losses on this particular occasion, the men of the herring town were well up to their southern rivals and had a little superfluous energy left over for carrying on a "sort of war" with their more immediate neighbours at Gorleston and elsewhere along the East Anglian coast. Any Portsman who took his ship to Yarmouth unaccompanied about this time had to keep a sharp look out if he was not to suffer the fate of the *Pekok* of Romney, which was sent to the bottom with her crew of thirty men. Nor did the men of Yarmouth confine their depredations to their own coast; the *Bayard* and four other ships of that port on their way to Gascony fell in with three fishing boats from Dover and promptly sank them; the *Godyer* of Yarmouth pursued the *Chivaler* of Dover from Swyne, over-took her, slew Absalom Ponyng, the master, and several of the crew, and plundered her cargo; at the Isle of Olerun Edmund Spitesale and others assaulted two boats from Hythe, and at la Colette, in Poitou, some Yarmouth men, finding the crew of the *St. Thomas* of Rye in a tavern, set upon them, slew five and maimed another, knocking out four of his teeth and cutting off his thumb. Against this we may set the action of the master of the *Shrimpe*, of Sandwich, in dragging a burgess of Yarmouth out of a church in Brittany and killing

More Medieval Byways

him. In the same way we may set off against one another the sinking and plundering of a Dover cog as she lay at Hartlepool taking in stores for the King's army in Scotland, and the seizure by a small squadron of piratical portsmen of the Bishop of Dublin's wool, in charge of Simon Fourapeni, of Yarmouth.

The origin of all this ill-feeling was the control exercised by the bailiffs of the Cinque Ports over the herring fair at Yarmouth, and in 1300, when the bailiffs were going in procession with their horn-blower and standard-bearer to the fair the townsmen rushed upon them, assaulted the horn-blower, dragged the standard-bearer off his horse, cutting off one of its ears, trampled the King's flag under foot, and tore it in pieces and drove the bailiffs out of the town. Nearly fifty years earlier in 1254, there had been a notable affray when King Henry, in a well-meant endeavour to avoid creating bad feeling, had arranged for the Queen to cross to France in a ship of Yarmouth, and Prince Edward in one of Winchelsea. Unfortunately, the Norfolk ship was much more elaborately got up, and no doubt the Yarmouth men boasted of its superiority, as the portsmen lost their tempers and destroyed the ship with all its finery. The moral of which is that it is better to be good than beautiful. And certainly it is probable that the ordinary passenger boat in medieval times offered few attractions beyond sea-worthiness. William Wey, writing in the middle of the fifteenth century, and referring to the boats plying between Venice and the Holy Land, advises the intending traveller, " Furste, yf ye goo in a galey make youre covenaunte by tyme wyth the patrone and chese yow a place in the seyd galey in the overest stage ; for in the lowyst under hyt ys ryght smolderyng hote and stynkyng." And a contemporary rhymester gives much the same impression of the accommodation provided on the boats plying at Santiago :

> " A sak of strawe were there ryght good,
> For som must lyg them in theyr hood ;
> I had as lefe be in the wood
>   Without mete or drynk ;
> For when that we shall go to bedde
> The pumpe was nygh our beddes hede,
> A man were as good to be dede
>   As smell thereof the stynk ! "

Nor was it sufficient to make arrangements to be " in a good honeste plase and to have yowre ese in the galey, and also to be cheryschet," there was the question of feeding to be considered, and the traveller was advised to insist " that yowre patrone yeff yow every day hote mete twyes at too melys, in the morninge at dyner and after none at soper." And although the commissariat might be plentiful, it did not follow that the quality would be up to the quantity, and as the wise traveller of the present day carries with him, or more especi- ally with her, a tin of biscuits, so did the provident pilgrim of medieval times, " ordeygne yowre byscokte to have wyth yow ; for thow ye schall be at the tabyl wyth yowre patrone, notwythstond- ynge ye schal oft tyme have nede to yowre vytelys, bred, chese, eggys, frute and bakyn, wyne and other, to make yowre collasyun ; for sum tyme ye schal have febyl bred, wyne and stynkyng water." For which reasons it was well to take a barrel of water and one of wine and, in view of the habits of pilgrims and sailors, it was just as well to keep both barrels in a chest with other stores under lock and key. The more luxurious passenger would also take care to lay in a good store of fruits and spices, " confectyunnys, comfortatyvys, laxatyvys and restoratyvys," while the complete traveller's outfit would include, beside a feather bed, which would cost three ducats when new, and could be re-sold for half that amount at the end of the voyage, a " lytyl cawdren and fryyng pan," with plates, dishes and glasses. As an afterthought William Wey adds the advice to buy " a cage for half a dosen of hennys or chekyn to have wyth yow in the galey." So equipped, the traveller need not fear any shortage of provisions, and could rest with equanimity while his ship lay becalmed, " walterynge and walowynge in the see." But, for all his frying pans and his chickens, he must have had a bad time when he encountered such weather as befell certain pilgrims returning from Palestine in the winter of 1506, when " there rose a wondre grete tempeste of excedynge moche wynde, and therewithall it rayned and hayled so unmesurably that no man myght loke forthe above the hatches, by force of the whiche tempest we were fayne to stryke all our sayles and droffe in the see as God wolde ; and what for the grete crye and noyse of the maryners and galyottes and for the noyse and syght of the idyous and ferefull storme and tempest, there was no man that toke any rest that nyght." It is true that the learned Gomesius propounds as a cure for melancholy " at seasonable times to be seasick " ; but such a remedy is ultra-heroic—it is, surely, to take not a hair but the whole hide of the dog which bit you—and my sympathy is with those whom " the wroughte sees tossyd and rolled ryght grevously."

If the passengers sometimes provided themselves with poultry it was also incumbent upon the ship-men to supply certain other live stock, and it was stipulated when the *Anne* of Hull was chartered for a fishing vogage to the Isle of Man in 1532, that the owner should find " a dog and a cat with all other necessaryes." The cat was, I suppose, to catch the rats and mice on board, the importance of the medieval mouser being shown not only by the doubtfully ancient tale of Lord Mayor Whittington and his cat, but much more emphatically by the early Welsh laws of Howel Ddha, one of which condemned the slayer of a cat to give in amends as much heaped grain as would cover its body when held up by the tail. With the exception of the wild species, which occurs often enough classed with foxes and hares as vermin of the chase, the cat figures very rarely in medieval records, though it plays a prominent part in folk-lore, and many early writers have left more or less accurate descriptions, usually unflattering, of its habits, including the fact, which most town-dwellers can sadly corroborate, that " he maketh a rueful noyse and ghastful when one proffereth to fight with another." What precisely the dog was doing on the ship, I do not know, unless he was there to exercise the cat, but his presence was occasionally important as, in the case of a wreck, if a dog or any other living creature remained on board, or escaped alive, the ship was not derelict, and its cargo did not count as wreck, but might be reclaimed by the owners, subject to paying for its salvage. It is to be feared, however, that there were few parts of the coast where the inhabitants would have scrupled to make away with a dog, or even a sailor, whose survival would deprive them of plunder, and when a ship drove ashore it was more a question of who could grab than of whose the goods might be. The wreckers of our sea coast might have pleaded immemorial precedent for their custom of looting, but they preferred not to plead at all, and for the legitimate " right of wreck " the Crown was particular to insist upon the production of charters. A curious custom existed in the thirteenth century at Seaford, where the port—for it then had a port, which afterwards moved westward to Newhaven—was divided between Peter of Savoy and William de Warenne, Earl of Surrey. In the port was a rock called " Wasbetel," and west of this all wreck belonged to the Earl ; eastwards it belonged to Peter, save that the Earl had anything which could be covered by a hatchet thrown by a man standing on the rock, who, at the moment of throwing, should with his left hand hold part of his hair below his right ear and should not in throwing bring his right hand above his left elbow.

Wrecking and piracy were the most common and profitable accessories to fishing in the pre-smuggling days, and the men of the Cinque Ports, with their semi-naval traditions, were probably the most villainous of all the English seamen who robbed and plundered foreigners with a complete disregard for truces and treaties, and kept their hands in by attacking each other when no foreigner was available. The yearly losses sustained by merchants through piracy cannot be calculated, but must have reached astonishing figures. When any particularly flagrant case or series of cases occurred the sufferers protested, and if their demands were not satisfied recompensed themselves by seizing the goods of any compatriots of the pirates, and leaving them to settle matters with the original aggressors. So in 1404, when the English fleet ran across three Genoese carracks, and "after longe bekeringe" took them and brought them into Winchelsea, when the "marchauntes Januence" found that they could not get either their ships or their merchandise back they "borrowed cloth, wolle and other merchaundises, amountynge unto great and notable summes, of dyverse merchauntes of Englande and sodenly avoyded the lande and lefte the foresayd notable summes unpayd, to the great hynderaunce and utter undoynge of many Englysshe merchauntes." Contrariwise in 1458, when the Genoese robbed the ship of Robert Sturmy, ex-Mayor of Bristol, either because he "hadde gotten grene pepyr and other spycys to have sette and sowen in Englande," or for other reasons, all the Genoese merchants in London were arrested and cast into the Fleet. But the number of cases in which retribution was exacted must have been small indeed compared with those which went unpunished, and the question of piracy must have been complicated by the practice of privateering, the privateer, or licensed pirate, not being over careful in discriminating between the subjects of friendly and of hostile princes.

Probably few privateers ever made such a haul as did that good Devon man, Robert Winnington, when in the spring of 1449 he met with a fleet of a hundred great ships of the Low Countries in the

Channel and promptly " cam abord the Admirall
and bade them stryke in the Kyngys name of
England ; and they bade me skyte in the Kyngys
name of England ; and then I and my feleschyp
sayd, but he wyll streke dow the sayle, that I wyld
over sayle hem by the grace of God, and God wyll
send me wynd and wether ; and dey bade me do
my wurst by cause I had so few schyppys and so
smale that they scornyd with me." But when it
came to the point they climbed down and sur-
rendered, after a bit of a fight, and he brought the
whole lot to the Isle of Wight, and, in view of the
injury they had done, he decided in cold blood " to
droune them and slee them, withoute that we hafe
tydyngs from our soverayn the Kyng and hys
counsell." Such methods of getting rid of enemies
were common enough, and what prisoners might
expect was shown in the case of a French gentle-
woman who was found in a Scottish ship by Lord
Scales' sailors. The latter " toke and departed
hir goodes amonges them and wolde have cast hir
ovyr the borde into the see, but as she prayed that
yf ther were any gentilman amonges them that she
might be put into his governaunce to save her
undefouled," and, as luck would have it, one
Thomas Beve was found who, after a good deal of
persuasion, did save her and a Carthusian friar,
confessor to the Duchess of Burgundy, whom the
sailors also wished to throw overboard. But while
a good many victims must have met their death
in this way, the greater number of prisoners were
no doubt put to ransom, and so regular a feature of
fishing life on the south-east coast was this that
in 1412 a scale of ransoms was drawn up for use
between the English and French, a master paying

six nobles, and twenty pence a week for board, and mariners paying the same amount for board, but only half the ransom, while boats and tackle were to be restored for forty pence. It is to be feared that at this time the French and their allies got quite as much out of the English at this game as we did out of them, for in spite of our theoretical sovereignty of the sea, it must be admitted that from the middle of the fourteenth century we were so far from ruling the waves that life on the sea coast was precarious, and even death was deprived of its privileges, the inhabitants of St. Senan's, in Cornwall, basing their demand for a church and cemetery of their own on the fact that the dead often could not be carried to the mother church of St. Buryan for fear of hostile incursions. So also, in the year of Agincourt, the men of Exmouth sought leave to build a church, because if they went to Budleigh to service pirates might seize and burn the town. Under the feeble rule of Henry VI matters grew even worse, and the enemy became " so bold that they kom up to the lond and pleyn here on Caster Sonds and in other plases, as homely as they were Englysch men." Nor were protective measures always a complete success, as in 1397 Abbotsbury Abbey complained that their estates on the coasts were harassed by Spaniards, Normans and Bretons, and that when men-at-arms were quartered there for their defence they consumed all the convent's stores, and carried off the cattle, so that the land was left untilled and the monks reduced to beggary, their last state being worse than their first.

VIII. Pilgrims ∽ ∽ ∽ ∽ ∽

ADMIRATION for those greater or better than ourselves is one of the most amiable characteristics of the human race, and one result of this pleasing trait is that places and objects in any way connected with our heroes become in themselves admirable, or at least interesting. How natural this is may be seen from the fact that it can be explained in two totally distinct and contradictory ways. Either man is so essentially materialistic that he must visit the Forum at Rome and see the spot where Cæsar fell in order to stimulate his imagination to grasp the fact of Cæsar's existence, or, on the other hand, he is so essentially spiritual that a subtle emanation issuing from the hero invests his surroundings and belongings with something of his own greatness, so that we may catch a faint reflection of zeal from the walls of Savonarola's cell, or of humour from the desk at which Dickens wrote the Pickwick Papers. On either hypothesis it is natural, and even laudable, that the Mohammedan should visit Mecca, the Christian the Holy Sepulchre, and the literary man Stratford-on-Avon. On the spiritual hypothesis the last might be the least satisfactory, if we could swallow the eccentric theories of those strange people, the Baconians, according to whom our reverence to the shrine of Shakespeare is as misplaced as the honour done by the deaf American, in a story more than middle-aged, if not positively medieval, to the relics of dead Milton (for him inglorious if not mute) under the impression that they belonged to that very " live " man, Lipton. It must, indeed, be admitted that if the virtue of a pilgrimage shrine lay in the odic force, or whatever the effluence be, shed upon it by its patron, some of the medieval pilgrims can have gotten little good for their pains. Of the thousand and one holy places visited by pilgrims to the Holy Land, not a few required a robuster faith than could be found at the present time. That a single cave should have served as the family vault of Abraham and Sarah, Isaac, Rebecca, Jacob and Leah, is conceivable, but that it should also have contained the bones of Adam and Eve is a large demand upon our credulity, even when supported by the proximity of another cave in which the form of the beds of Adam and Eve could still be seen in the fifteenth century. " The statu of salt of Lothes wyffe, by sydes the deed see " was more of a curio than a relic, and was judiciously omitted by Sir Richard Guylford's chaplain on the ground that " that place standeth so that it is very laborious to se," but the birthplace of Elijah and the house of Dives were duly admired, and the worthy man seems to have found no difficulty in visiting on successive days the place where the tree grew that was cut down to form the Holy Cross, and the place where in the days of the Queen of Sheba a torrent was bridged by a tree afterwards destined to form that same Holy Cross.

I do not know what the official attitude of the Church was towards some of these clearly fictitious shrines, but presumably it was considered more important that the deeds of the saints and worthies should be called to mind than that they should be

localised with the accuracy of the modern historian.
Certainly the Church never countenanced the
belief that everything asserted to be a relic was
genuine, even if she did put the seal of her approval
on some of more than doubtful authenticity.
There could be no disputing such relics as the
broken point of the sword with which St. Thomas
of Canterbury was slain ; nor was there much reason
to doubt the genuineness of the body of St. Wilfrid
at Ripon, but on the other hand the other body of
that same saint preserved at Canterbury was open
to grave doubts. Even with the relics of the
earliest days of the Faith there was room for
classification ; the Holy Coat of Treves was, in
itself, an object quite likely to have been treasured
and preserved, while the tablecloth used at the
Last Supper, exhibited at the Lateran, was almost
as inconceivable a relic as the " hey that Cryst lay
in before the asse," which was kept at Sta. Maria
Maggiore, and even this latter is reasonable beside
the milk of the Blessed Virgin shown at several
English monasteries. The cathedral priory of
Rochester in the thirteenth century surpassed
its rivals by possessing not only Aaron's rod
(another of his rods was at the Lateran), but " part
of the rod of Moses, which budded "—though upon
what occasion it so budded the monkish chronicler
did not record. Here also, was " some of the earth
from which God fashioned Adam," but this was not
so scarce an object as might be supposed, for about
a bowshot from the family vault of Abraham was
" Ager Damascenus, in the whiche place Adam was
made. This Ager Damascenus hath erth moche
inclynynge to red, and is flexible and toughe as wex,
the whiche erthe the Sarrasyns dygge in grete

plenty and lede it into Egypte, Ethyop, and Inde, and there they sells it very dere for golde and spyces; and the pyttes that they dygge for the same erthe be full ayen, and is as playne grounde as any other within the same valey within the space of a yere without any castinge in or helpe of mannes hande. And who so ever beryth of the same erthe uppon hym is saffely assured from noyeng of any beste, and it kepeth a man frome the fallynge evyll."

Of the English centres of pilgrimage it goes without saying that Canterbury came first. Walsingham was a good second, and probably St. Albans might be placed third, but there were endless lesser centres. Apart from special shrines it was the custom in most dioceses for representatives of all the parishes to come together to the cathedral church on some particular saint's day, carrying crosses and banners and staves, which served not only to adorn the processions, but also, at Chichester, to break the heads of rival parishioners who attempted to secure a position in the procession which they were not strong enough to keep. In this same diocese, in consideration of the fact that Chichester was at the extreme west, permission was given to the pilgrims to visit instead Lewes in the centre, or Hastings at the east. The latter was in itself a small centre of pilgrimage, and we find Edward II when stopping at Pevensey Castle in 1325, kindly paying the expenses of " little Will Fisher " going on a pilgrimage to Hastings. It was on this same occasion that King Edward gave money to " a poor old man telling tales of the siege of the castle by Sir Simon de Montfort," and we would give a good deal more than the King gave to have those tales recorded. The elder Simon de

Montfort, the great Earl of Leicester, himself became an uncanonised saint, and drew no few pilgrims to his wonder-working tomb at Evesham, and with him might be classed Richard, Earl of Arundel, Thomas, Earl of Lancaster, and Archbishop Scrope. And seeing that his partisans actually ascribed miracles and saintliness to that unprincipled young blackguard, Henry, son of Henry II, who died of a fever caught when robbing the shrine of Rochamadour, it is not surprising that the tomb of the harmless King Henry VI should have become an object of mild devotion, though it was unfortunate for Thomas Clerk, of Nottinghamshire, that he should have gone on pilgrimage thither, as he ran up against William Phelip, "which ought him malice and ill will," and caused him to be arrested as a vagabond, and cast into prison, where he remained for sixteen weeks or more.

The influence of all these shrines drawing their streams, small or great, of pilgrims, must have been greater than most historians have realised. Not only did Canterbury wax fat at the expense of her pious visitors, but so did Dartford, Rochester and Ospringe, the usual sleeping-places on the road from London, and all the wayside inns where the less ascetic pilgrims might, with Chaucer's Pardoner, "byten on a cake" and drink "a draught of corny ale." The Reformation must have been as serious a blow to many innkeepers as the coming of the railways was to their descendants in the country posting-houses, and from it must be dated the parochial insularity which characterised the English peasant of the last two centuries. Canterbury and St. Albans survived, or recovered from the loss of their pilgrims, but of many a once busy district it might be said, as was said of Walsingham :

> " Oules do scrike where the sweetest himenes
>   Lately were songe.
> Toades and serpents hold ther dennes
>   Where the palmers did throng."

One pilgrimage in Britain still retains its ancient fame, and as, in 1285 on St. Clement's Day, five men of Cambridge gathered in church to have their staves and purses hallowed for a pilgrimage to St. Andrew's, in Scotland, so now may you find many times five Cambridge men with their staves and purses setting forth to St. Andrew's, but it is to be feared that their staves are unhallowed ; and who indeed would bless staves with such outlandish names as mashies, cleeks, and niblicks ? But far be it from me to suggest that a medieval pilgrimage was a frivolous matter to be lightly undertaken. It certainly was not when St. James of Compostella was the goal, as it so often was :

> " Men may leve alle gamys
>   That saylen to Saynt Jamys !
> For many a man it gramys,
>   When they begyn to sayle.
> For when they have taken the see
> At Sandwyche or at Wynchylsee,
> At Bristow, or where that hit bee,
>   Theyr hartes begyn to fayle."

The pilgrim ships must have been desperately uncomfortable, and when the weather was bad the unfortunate passengers must have wished that they had chosen some other form of penance, for sea-sickness is no modern ailment (there was a manor in Kent held by the unpleasant tenure of holding the King's head when he crossed the Channel) :

> " Thys mene whyle the pylgryms ly,
> And have theyr bowlys fast theym by,
> And cry aftyr hot malvesy
>   Theyr helthe for to restore.
> And som wold have a salted tost,
> For they myght ete neyther sode nor rost ;
> A man myght sone pay for theyr cost,
>   As for oo day or twayne.
> Som layde theyr bookys on theyr kne
> And rad so long they myght nat se ;—
> ' Allas ! myne hed woll cleve on thre ! '
>   Thus saythe another certayne."

And yet, if we may believe Andrew Borde, the sea journey to Santiago was far better than that by land. Even the pilgrimage to Canterbury was not without its perils, and the lonely traveller was liable to be snapped up by lurking robbers, as Chaucer's Host feared the drunken cook would be when he dropped behind. But at least one pilgrim would have done better to risk the robbers and travel alone, for when Alice, wife of William Willard, of Rotherfield, set out for Canterbury, her servant Ducea, and her companion, Alice of Wadhurst, strangled her, at Frant, by her husband's orders. Still such happenings were rare, and beyond being fleeced by a crowd of hermits, friars, monks and nuns, the pilgrim to Canterbury or any other English shrine had usually little to fear. It was another matter when visiting the Holy Land. Of course many early pilgrims relied on their arms ; they were, in fact, the crusaders, and we have an interesting note of the equipment

of a Cornish crusader, Robert de Marisco, in 1202.
His father provided him with a horse, a coat of
mail, a pair of iron greaves, a helmet and sword,
a scarlet cloak, a gold ring, and 20 marks and 32
besants in money. The dangers of the journey
did not deter even women from going to Palestine,
and in 1330 we find Maud de Bionie, of London,
setting out on what may be called the grand tour
of the religious world, to visit the Holy Sepulchre,
Santiago and Assisi. Unfortunately, soon after
leaving Valence, her boat upset in the Rhone,
several of her companions were drowned, and
although saved herself, she lost all her money,
and had to abandon her pilgrimage and enter a
convent. Possibly she was more fortunate than
she knew, for Isabel Parewastel, who got back to
Bridgwater in 1366 after three years in the Holy
Land, suffered severely at the hands of the Saracens, being on one occasion stripped, and placed
head downwards on a rack and beaten. It was
only a few years later that Thomas Burton was
made prisoner in the same way, and his wife, Joan,
having converted all her lands and goods into cash,
went on a ship at Gravesend to go out and ransom
him, and was then arrested for taking bullion out
of the country, which was hard luck. Even more
dangerous than the voyage to Jerusalem was a
visit to Mount Sinai, where St. Catherine was
buried by the angels, and it is significant that
when William de Kilverby, canon of Lincoln, and
an especial devotee of St. Catherine, obtained a
papal indult to visit that shrine in 1339, he was
enjoined to take with him nothing that could be
of use to the pagans, the supposition evidently
being that he would fall into their hands. Fortu-

nately for those who, like Sir Christopher Palla-
vicini in 1506, " founde that passage so dangerous,
fyndynge no sure conduyte, that he durste aventure
no further that way than to Cayre " (that is to
say, Cairo, where, if we may believe Burton, good
pilgrims to Mecca were wont to eat a camel), the
proverb of Mahomet and the mountain was
reversed, and the mountain, or at least its spiritual
privileges, came to the pilgrims. It was within a
couple of years of Sir Christopher's disappoint-
ment that Peter de Casanova, deputy of Saba
Cirus, monk of St. Catherine's on Mount Sinai,
came over to England to distribute broadcast, to
such of the faithful as would pay for them, letters
of pardon. In London he hired Robert Grene, at
2s. a week, to ride with him to York and elsewhere,
but there seems to have been little enthusiasm for
the fraternity of St. Catherine, and Robert's wages
were left unpaid. Failing to get his arrears in
cash, Robert took sixteen hundred letters of
pardon, for which he agreed to pay the nominal
fee of 10 marks, and set off to make what he could
out of them. He appears to have found a few
parochial clergy who were willing to act as sub-
agents, and with them he left batches of pardons
for disposal, but when he got to Alnwick the men
of the north country showed their opinion of
pardoners by kicking him out of the town and
compelling him to eat one of his own letters of
pardon, which, however good it may have been
for his soul, proved bad for his body and made
him very ill. The priest who had gone surety for
the 10 marks was also pretty sick.

But if dangers arose from pilgrimages, still more
pilgrimages sprang from dangers. Whence it

sometimes happened that one pilgrimage led to many. When Sir Richard Guylford's retinue returned from Palestine, leaving their master and the prior of Guisborough dead in the Holy City, in the winter of 1506, their galley met with such a succession of " grate outrageous stormes " that not only did the individual pilgrims make a score of vows, but on two occasions the whole of the ship's crew and passengers vowed united pilgrimage. On the first occasion, when their anchors were dragging and their boat drifting on the rocks of the " yle of Mylo," they " all yave money and vowed a pylgrymage in generall to our blessed Lady de Myraculis at Venyse," while on the second occasion, when their " moste noyaunce and ferefull grefe was that we had no porte nor havyn to flee to for socoure and herborowe but into Turkey or Barbary, into the handes of the Infidels," they " all by one assent avowed a pylgrymage to be made in all our behalffes to our blessed Lady of Loreta, besyde Anchona in Italye, and deputed certayne pylgrymes to gather the money amonges us to make the costes and laboure of a pylgryme to be sent in our names with our offerings." Perils of land also involved vows, and at the battle of Agincourt two Welshmen, Thomas Bassegle, of Cardiff, and John Williams, of Howell, vowed to visit Our Lady of Walsingham if they came through safely. But, look you, though they survived the battle they were arrested at Sawston on their way to Walsingham, and imprisoned in Cambridge Castle, indeed they were, whateffer !

Of all perils, however, none was so frequent a cause of pious vows as sickness, and one of the most delightful of Margaret Paston's letters to her husband, after declaring that " be my trowthe my moder and I were nowth in hertys fro the tyme that we woste of your sekenesse tyl we woste verely of your amendyng," goes on—" My moder behested anodyr ymmage of wax of the weytte of yow to ouer Lady of Walsyngham, and sche sent iiij nobyls to the iiij Orderys of Frerys at Norweche to pray for yow, and I have behested to gon on pylgreymmays to Walsingham, and to Saint Levenardys (at Norwich) for yow." Conversely, just a century earlier, Sir Peter de Thornton, when his wife was ill, vowed to go to Jerusalem ; but when she recovered he himself was too infirm to go, and he was therefore allowed to contribute the cost of his journey to the Holy Land subsidy instead. Such commutations of vows were not uncommon, as the intended journey often proved to be impossible for some reason ; either the would-be pilgrims were " too old at forty " as in the case of Elizabeth de Burgh, Lady of Clare, who in 1343 was absolved from her vow to visit the Holy Land and Santiago because " being now forty she cannot hope to do so " ; or there were difficulties, as with Dame Margaret Naunton, who vowed, at the desire of her first husband, to visit Santiago, but was excused on account of her age, the number of her children, and the opposition of her second husband. The expenses of the proposed journey had usually in such cases to be devoted to some pious object, and often an extra penance was enjoined, but it cannot have been often that consciences were as tender as those of William Creswick, a worthy citizen of London, and his wife Alice. It seems that in their ardent youth both had made vows, he to visit the Holy Sepulchre, and she Rome, but, possibly because they fell in love and put such matters out of each other's head, they postponed their pilgrimages and got married. Then they found, as many have found since then, that trips abroad are not so lightly undertaken when you are married, so William went to the papal legate, and by virtue of contributing to the churches of Canterbury and London, was absolved from his vow. Feeling that they had perhaps got off too cheaply they next sent out proxies, one to Jerusalem and one to Rome ; but still they were not happy, so they invoked the aid of the papal nuncio, who re-absolved them, in consideration of a payment to the church of Rome. Years passed and they determined to make things sure, so they laid their case before the Pope himself, who ordered them to assign to the repair of the churches of Rome a sum equal to the estimated expenses of their intended journeys and offerings. Let us hope they were content with that.

Innate piety and pressing danger were not the only causes of pilgrimages, for, as some achieve greatness and some have greatness thrust upon them, so some had pilgrimages thrust upon them by way of penance. So, for instance, Bishop Rede sent the Vicar of Walberton off to walk to Rome to obtain absolution for having taken violent measures to ensure the chaplain of Slindon keeping his vow of chastity. The same bishop packed off the constable of Arundel Castle and half-a-dozen other offenders to St. Richard's shrine at Chichester, barefoot, for arresting a thief who had got hold of the handle of Arundel Church. Commonest of all pilgrimages was the brief but unpleasant tour so many times round the parish church, accompanied

More Medieval Byways

by the parish priest or his deputy, bearing, and applying, the rod of correction. Such little penitential tours were usually undertaken in company with one of the other sex, and it is noteworthy that—at any rate in Durham—the man usually received more punishment than his partner in guilt ; but, of course, that was many centuries ago — *nous avons changé tout cela*. On such occasions the penitents were ordered to appear in their shifts, but Agnes Hebburne, whom I should like to identify with that Agnes who dwelt with " Helen of Hell " (*de Inferno*), took her oath that she had not got a decent shift, and could not afford to buy one, so the judge told her to do her penance in a tunic, and " the garment called *le napron* (an apron)." It was " in lynen apparell " that Charles Shaw stood up in the church of St. Nicholas, Durham, and publicly expressed his sorrow for having called Bertram Mitford " a covitous snowge," and certain other offensive, but less pleasing terms. Some of his contemporaries showed a remarkable fluency of abuse, one of them calling a priest " a vacobounde, a wagwallet, and a syde-tayled knave," while an epithet that led to an exchange of blows was " Scots mongrel," the offence lying not in the " mongrel " but in the " Scots." It is strange to think that an Englishman should ever have brought a libel action against a man for calling him a Scot. I wonder what penance would now meet the case of a southerner who dared to suggest that Scot was a term libellous in itself ? Possibly a pilgrimage to St. Andrew's, visiting the eighteen holy stations in company with two or three outspoken Scottish caddies might be deemed suitable.

IX. "With Trumpets also and Shawms"

"ALL sounds (as the philosopher observes) arise from the quick and nimble elision or percussion of the air, being either divided by the lips or reeds of pipes, hautboys, flutes or other wind instruments, or else struck and put into motion by the tremulous vibration of strings, yielding an agreeable sound to the ear." Without carping at the philosopher's apparent belief that all sounds produced from wind or string instruments are pleasing, it may well be objected that he has not given proper honour to the instruments of pure percussion, such as the cymbals, sistrum and tinkling triangle and all the martial host of drums, tabors, and nakers. Thus Jubal, father of all harpers, fiddlers, crowders, lyrists, lutists, players upon the psaltery, dulcimer, clavichord, virginals, rebek and theorbo and all twangsters in general, is unduly exalted above his half-brother Tubal Cain. Unduly, because it was Tubal Cain, earliest of harmonious blacksmiths, who by the clanging of three proportioned hammers upon his anvil first regulated the consonances, with the assistance of Pythagoras,—according to one anachronicler,—and ensured the perpetuation of his discovery against cataclysms of fire or flood by engraving his theory upon tablets of clay and of bronze. Perhaps it was after the Deluge (which Tubal Cain had foreseen) that Mercury, wandering over the fields of Egypt, found among the other drowned beasts, a snail "and when the snaylle was rostyd"—

whether by Mercury for his lunch, or, as I suppose, by the rays of the sun—" the synewes left and were streyned in the sneylle's house. And Mercurius smote the synewes and of them came a sowne." Pleased with the sound, the industrious god constructed a lyre on the plan of the snail shell and gave it " to one that was namyd Orpheus, which was moost besy abowtte such thinges." What good, or at least remarkable, use Orpheus made of it is well known, and if any are so sceptical as to doubt his traditional performances they will surely reconsider their opinions in the light of the experience of " the famous Mr. John Playford," the great music publisher of the seventeenth century, who relates " That himself once travelling near Royston met a herd of stags, about twenty, upon the road, following a bagpipe and violin ; when the music played they went forward, when it ceased they all stood still ; and in this manner they were conducted out of Yorkshire to the King's palace at Hampton Court."

Long before Mr. Playford's days Trevisa wrote that " musyk excyteth and comfortyth bestes and serpentes, foules and delphines to take hede thereof." Moreover, he also noted the fondness of deer for the pipe—possibly to be accounted for by the first pipes having been formed from the leg-bones of harts : " Hunters usyth this instrument, for hartes lovyth the noyse thereof. But whyle the harte taketh hede and likynge in the pypynge of an hunter, another hunter, whiche he hath no knowlage of, cometh and shoteth at the harte and sleeth hym. Pypyng begyleth byrdes and foules. therefore it is sayd ' the pype syngeth swetely whyle the fowler begyleth the byrd.' And shepe loveth pypynge, therfore shepherdes usyth pypes when they walke wyth thyr shepe."

And if the modern shepherd's pipe is to be seen and smelt rather than heard, at any rate the goatherd of Paris still leads his flock through the streets of the old city to the music of the traditional pipe of Pan—or did in the years before the war.

Turn we now from beasts to men, alike as performers and audience. "Comforte of voys pleasyth and comfortyth the hert and inwyttes in alle dysease and traveylle of werks and werynesse." But pleasant as it is, in most people's opinion, to listen to a good soloist, at least one early musician considered that such a performance was incomplete and much inferior to a good glee, chant, canon, chorus, roundelay, madrigal or part song. "Alle melodye nedeth many voys, for one voys plesith not so much as the voys and songe of the cuckoe"; at the same time "If many dyscordith the voys plesith not; for of suche dyscorde comyth not songe but howlynge other (or) yellynge." To lessen the risk of such discords it is essential not only to grasp the significance of diastema, diesis, tonus, iperludius, podorius, arsis, thesis, dyatesseron, dyapente, and the sexquitercia proporcio, things "in themselfe deepe and full mystyk, derk to understondynge," but also to know the different kinds of voices which have to be dealt with. "Voyces ben smalle, subtill, thicke, clere, sharpe and shylle. In subtylle voys the spyryte is not strong, as in children and in wymmen, and in other that have not grete synews, strong and thycke; for of smalle strynges cometh smalle voys and subtyll."

More Medieval Byways

Such a voice had Louis XII, who, being fond but ignorant of music, mightily disconcerted his chapel master, Jusquin des Prés, by ordering him to compose a piece in which he himself might take one part. Jusquin rose to the occasion and wrote a canon for two boys' voices, assigning the king to hold a single note " in a pitch proper for a Contratenor," further assisting his royal master's grip on that one note by himself singing a bass part in which every alternate note was the octave of the king's note. Of thick and clear voices the clear—contrary to the case with soup—is superior. " The voyces ben fatte and thycke whan moche spyryte comyth owt, as the voys of a man. The voys is clere that sowynth well and ryngeth wythout any hollownesse. Sharpe voyces ben full hyghe, shylle voyces ben lowde and drawth a longe and fylleth soone alle the place, as the noyce of trumpes. The harde voys is horse, and also the harde voys is grymme and grysely whan the sowne therof is vyolente, and as the sowne of thondre and of a felde (anvil) bete with grete malles. The rough voys is horse and sparplyd by smalle, and is styffyd and dureth not longe, as the sowne of erthen vessell."

It must have been a hard and rough voice that the clerk of a Sussex parish possessed, whose epitaph, as written in the register, recorded that when he sang his voice " warbled forth as if he had been thumped on the back with a stone." On the other hand, " the perfyghte voys is hyghe, swete, stronge and clere ; hyghe to be well herde, clere to fyll the eeres, swete to pleyse and not to fere the herynge and to comfort the hertes to take hede thereto."

"With Trumpets also and Shawms"

Such a voice had Taliesen of the radiant brow, before whom the four and twenty bards of Maelgwn Gwynnedd became as drunken stammerers; and some such qualities must his successors, the Welsh bards, have had, though Andrew Borde makes his Welshman declare:

"My songe and my voyce and my harpe doth agree,
Muche lyke the hussynge of a homble bee."

A great man was the Welsh bard when he had been invested by the King with a harp worth ten shillings, and by the Queen with a gold ring. If he asked a favour of the King, he could pay for it with an ode, while a benefactor of lower rank could only demand to be sung to sleep. When the army was arrayed he sang the Song of the British Kings, and in reward received at the end of the foray an ox or a cow from the loot. Nor did he hesitate upon occasion to lend the force of his arm as well as the encouragement of his voice to the combatants. Adaon, son of the radiant Taliesin, was one of the three dauntless chieftains who feared nothing in the day of battle, and Gwrgant ap Rhys, "the best poet" of Morgan ap Owain, was slain with his master in 1157. In the same way the Norman minstrel Taillefer achieved death and immortality on the field of Hastings, singing the Song of Roland and charging the enemy single-handed.

The part played by minstrels and wandering "mewsecyons" in the Middle Ages must have been very much greater than is usually realised. The political songs and ballads which constitute a large portion of the surviving examples of purely

More Medieval Byways

popular literature, composed by the people for their own use, of the thirteenth to fifteenth centuries, must have been spread by these minstrels who chanted or declaimed them in the market places and village inns ; and it is probably no exaggeration to say that every important political movement during those centuries was preceded and accompanied by a flood of such rhymes and ballads. Not that it must be assumed that the minstrels were as a rule deliberate political agents. On the contrary, their first aim was to fill their pockets, or at least their stomachs, by appealing to the taste of their audience ; on occasions of political excitement, most of them were probably sufficiently skilled *improvisatori* to turn out rough rhymes in accordance with their listeners' demands, but generally ballads of Robin Hood or other less reputable heroes formed their stock-in-trade. The wording was often clumsy, the humour broad and heavy, and the singing erratic, but it was at least more intelligible to the hearers than any high-faluting operatic performance would have been,

> " For is it not as good to say playnly
> Gyf me a spade,
> As gyf me a spa-ue-ua-ue-ua-ue-uade ? "

Of course the better class of minstrels who performed in the houses of the wealthy, or attached themselves to the retinues of nobles, were often musicians of merit with good voices and a repertory of romantic poems of love and chivalry, from which they were wont to

> " Maken harpynge in many place
> Of Octavyan and Ysambrace,

"With Trumpets also and Shawms"

> And of many other gestes,
> Namely when thei come to festes,
> As o the lyf of Bevys of Hampton
> That was a Knyght of gret renoun."

Some idea of the popularity of minstrelsy as a
profession may be gathered from the fact that at
the marriage of the Princess Margaret in 1290 a
hundred pounds was distributed by the hands of
Walter de Storton, King Edward's harper, to 426
minstrels, English and foreign, who had come to the
ceremony, while nine years later at the marriage
of Edward I to Margaret of France at Canterbury,
John le Leutor and Dicky (*Ricardettus*) le Vylour
were entrusted with the distribution of £60 to
minstrels of France, and £40 to English, and in
1287 when King Edward spent Christmas at St.
Macaire he gave over £50 to 125 musicians.   The
account books of any royal or noble house show
alike   on   how   many   occasions   minstrels   and
players put in an appearance, and how lavishly
they were rewarded, especially when they had
the good fortune to be retainers of some great
person.   To   take   a   few   examples   at   random
from my notebooks, John the Trumpeter of Sir
Robert fitz Payn, who trumpeted before the King
on the Feast of the Epiphany, 1305, and the harper
of John Mautravers who harped on the same day,
were each rewarded with a gift of 20s., equivalent
to something like £15 of modern money.   Bonevye,
minstrel of Sir William de Fenes, was given 40s.
for playing at the marriage of Princess Margaret
in 1290, and the same amount was bestowed upon
Ernulph, fiddler and minstrel to the Count of
St. Pol, on the occasion of the marriage of Margaret's sister, Joan of Acre.   Forty shillings also

were given by Queen Eleanor to Robert de Bauneevil, minstrel of the King of France, by the hands of Philip, who was actor or player to Edmund Crouchback, and three years earlier, in 1287, King Edward gave as much as 50s. to Lepin, minstrel of Sir Ralph de Nesle, Constable of France, and also 40s. to Parassatus, minstrel and wait to Mar de Barsauma, Bishop of the East, ambassador of that interesting convert to Christianity, Argon, Khan of the Tartars, to whom Edward once sent an embassy, as has been related elsewhere.[1] That a minstrel was considered a reasonable, if not essential, member of an ambassador's retinue may be gathered from the circumstance that Gerlac de Gardinis, when sent from the English court on an embassy to the King of the Germans, claimed allowance for one esquire and one minstrel. Casual itinerant musicians, such as the " young man with a bagpipe " who piped to Edward I at Bordeaux at Easter, 1287, or his later counterpart, the " drone that plaed a song before the lordes " at Belvoir in 1539, lacking the reflected glory of a noble master, had naturally to be content with smaller rewards, but their takings were not inconsiderable, especially when compared with the amount of labour involved.

A parasitical life, yielding the highest returns to those most skilful in amusing their audience, at the expence often of decency and decorum, was not likely to tend to virtue or to escape the notice of the omnipresent moralist of the Middle Ages.

> " Immoral ditties are their delight ;
> Vain and tasteless praise they recite,

[1] See my *Medieval Byways*, Chapter II.

The Church and worship they do not heed ;
In idleness themselves they feed.
The birds do fly, the fish swim all,
The bees gather honey, the worms do crawl,
Everything works its food to obtain,
But minstrels and thieves make idle gain."

A sixteenth century platitudinarian, anticipating
the sentiments of a later puritanical generation,
asserted that " Instruments of mynstrelsy seldome
doth please God " ; on which subject it is possible
that David and other Old Testament worthies
might have expressed a different opinion ; and
adds, " a man that intendyth to mynstrels shall
soone be weddyd to poverte and his sonne shall
heryte derision." At the same time the good man
seems to have had a little secret shamefaced
sympathy with minstrelsy, for after giving the
warning that " He that lawith [laugheth] at a
minstrel's words gevith to hym a wedde [a pledge],"
he advises a compromise ; " Iff mynstrels please
thee, feyne as thow herde them not but thynke
uppone another." The attitude is not unknown
at the present day among self-conscious people who
take themselves seriously, and may be observed
at any humorous entertainment. The classification of minstrels and players as rogues and vagabonds is well known, and if any distinction was
made it was to the disadvantage of the players.
The eternal joy of dressing up, which has possessed
all child-hearted men and women from time
immemorial, has always been regarded with dis-
favour by superior people, and the eccentricities
of costume adopted by the mummers and players
constituted no small part of their offence in the
eyes of the dull and unimaginative framers of our

laws. Even worthy Master Fabyan in his account of the meeting between Edward IV and Louis XI says severely : " Of the nyse and wanton disgysyd apparayll that the Kynge Lowys ware upon hym at the tyme of thys meetynge I myght make a longe rehersayl ; but for it should sownde more to dishonour of suche a noble man, that was apparaylled more lyke a mynstrell than a prynce royal, therefor I passe it over. For albeit that he was so new fangyll in his clothinge, yet had he many vertues."

Yet Edward III did not disdain to appear in public with his knights disguised as Saracens, and his wardrobe at Guildford Castle the Christmas before the Pestilence would have been a joy to any house party in wet weather, including as it did forty-two masks of men, women and silvered angels' faces, and complete outfits for swans, peacocks and dragons. Even his martial grandfather had worn fancy dress in his youth, and in his maturer years was not above paying the tailor's bill for " queyntis," or fantastic costumes, for his daughter and his Gascon knights. That the second Edward was a devotee of theatricals need not increase our respect for the histrionic art, but can hardly decrease our respect for himself. In 1303, when Edward was still Prince of Wales, he spent the Christmas season at South Warnboro' and evidently organised some theatrical entertainments, as John Albon and two other painters came down from London to paint certain quaintisies for the Prince's games, and supplies of buckram, Aylesham cloth, silvered skins and twenty fathoms of wire were sent down " for the interludes made by the prince "—in which three clerks of Windsor took

part. Some two centuries later the players found
a notable patron in Henry VIII, who kept a company of actors. One of them was a certain George
Meller to whom on November 23, 1527, came
Thomas Arthure, desiring that he would " teiche
hyme playinge of Interludes " so that he might
also become one of the King's players. Thomas
was therefore enrolled as a super in Maller's
company for a year at fourpence a day, and his
board ; but he proved a bad bargain, for he was
" ryght harde and dull too taike any lernynge,
whereby he was nothinge meate or apte to bee in
service with the Kinge's grace too maike any plaies
or interludes before his highnes." Worse than his
density was his conduct, for after seven weeks he
absconded and persuaded three of Maller's servants, " beinge experte in playinge," to go with
him. The truants toured the provinces with a
success which suggests that Arthure was not such a
fool as his master made out, getting " greate availe,
profit and avauntage by reason of the forseide
interludes and plaies," which their dramatic
instructor felt ought to have fallen to him. To
add insult to injury Arthure sued Mellar for the
right to wear the King's badge and for a share in
the fees paid to the King's players, and as Mellar
happened to be in Ludgate prison at the time, the
case went against him.

Henry's daughter, the unhappy, but by no means
gloomy, Mary, seems to have inherited her father's
tastes to some extent, though it would be rash to
support this statement by referring to the interesting list of " costs and charges leyde owte and
payde by John Thurgoode, Lorde of Mysruel with
the Pryncess' grace in Crysmastyme the xiij yere

of the reigne of Kyng Henry the viii," which has survived, as Mary was at the time only six years old. Among these costs appear such items as 5s. 4d. paid " to a paynter of Wyndesore for making vysors, payntyng of Fasez, coote armors, hatts for dysgysyng" and 3s. 8d. " for hyre of garments, herys [which I suppose to be hairs, that is to say wigs] and hattys at London," small payments "for strawe that xij men were covered with in a disgysyng," "for making a payre of sloppys for Jakys when he played the chypman," and " to a man of Wyndesore for kyllyng of a calffe before my lades grace behynde a clothe." In the last entry the uncritical Protestant writers of an earlier generation would have seen precocious evidence of those tendencies which in later days saddled Mary with the epithet " Bloody," but it is probable that in reality the man of Windsor was paid for giving a lifelike imitation of calf-killing, and that the entry is no more to be taken literally than such entries as occur in connection with mystery plays, as —" for mendyng the devells cote," " for mendynge hellmowthe " or " for settynge the world of fyer." In passing it is worth noting that at Coventry the payment for " white soules " was 6d. a piece, for " blakke soules " and " wormes of conscience " 8d., these being probably walking-on parts, while a speaking part received more, though 1s. 4d. for " the sprytt of God " seems inadequate.

The prevalence in the Middle Ages, and even after the Reformation, of little companies of players, mummers and actors of interludes in the country districts is very well brought out in such early accounts as those of the Willoughbys at

Wollaton, or the Earls of Rutland at Belvoir, in
which are constantly recorded payments of small
sums " to vj men that played before my Master
an interlude," " to iiij plaers that plaed before the
ladies on Neweyers day," " to the playars of
Browton on Nowyers Ewyn," and so forth. That
it was possible to have too much of this form of
entertainment may be gathered from such entries
as " in reywarde to vj players of Derbbyshyre
weche played not xxd." or even more definitely
" to iij mensterrelles off Nottingham in reywarde
becawse they playd not xxd." Either Sir Francis
Willoughby had a better early morning temper
than most men or " Edlin the musission " was
an exceptional performer, that he should have been
rewarded with 5s., " for playing at my Master his
chamber dore on Newyeres daye." To be aroused
at an early hour on a winter's morning by strains
of alleged music does not tend to excite feelings
of generosity, and so it is not surprising that
serenaders (whose fatuity in standing on a snowy
winter's night below their lady's window, howling
like dogs, amazed even that connoisseur of fools,
Hans Geyler) should occasionally have met the
sloppy fate which befel St. Louis at the hands of
the early-rising student—and, in more recent
times, the Master of Pembroke, at the hands of a
learned scholar who shall remain anonymous. It
is not every one that appreciates the waits to the
extent of endorsing the opinion that " wyth pipes
watchynge men pleyseth suche men as restyth in
beddes and makyth them slepe the sooner and
more swetly by melodye of pypes." Nowadays
the waits are chiefly connected in our minds with
carols, a form of song which appears to be essen-

tially English, if we may accept the verdict of a German writer who classicised his name as " Ornithoparcus." In describing the various methods of singing in vogue among the nations of Europe he says : " The English do carroll ; the French sing ; the Spaniards weepe ; the Italians which dwell about the coasts of Janua caper with their voyces, other barke ; but the Germanes, which I am ashamed to utter, doe howle like wolves."

Even carolling might at times be alarming, and in 1312 the merchants of Louvain, Ghent, Dinant, Caen and other towns, the Bardi—most famous of Italian financiers—and the English merchants, laid a solemn and united protest against William de Scorborough, chaplain, Robert de Durham, Hugh de Wyteby, Edmund and Miles Pickard and others, to the effect that on Saturday, May 6, they came into the fair of St. Ives and carolled to the terror of the fair and the danger of the merchants. Some dozen years later the fair at Carnarvon was disturbed by the action of Robert of the Brewhouse, probably a taverner, in receiving into his house " les skirmisours," that is to say the scaramouches, merry-andrews or buffoons.

The enjoyment of buffoonery and horse-play, and the antics of fools, is not a mark of high intelligence, even when found in exalted ranks, and it is curious that Christian kings and nobles should have adopted the practice of keeping fools and half-witted persons in their retinue. Had this been done on the Egyptian principle of the skeleton at the feast, as a constant reminder of the folly of the wise and the limitations of human wisdom it would have been intelligible, but that these " innocents," whom the Saracens and other pagans treated with respect and tenderness, as being under God's special protection, should have been kept for mockery and laughter tempts one to exclaim with the medieval preacher, " Thou that jesteth with fools and delyghteth therein, buy thyself a mirror and whenever thou lookest therein thou shalt see a fool ; then laugh ! " That Edward II was one of those to whom this advice might have been given, and also one of the practical jokers who form the first subdivision of Geyler's sixty-seventh regiment of fools, appears from an entry of 4s. given " to Robert Buffard, fool, by reason of the ill-treatment that he sustained at the prince's hands in the water on 25 February." Another entry shows the impecunious prince giving the unusually lavish reward of 5s. to a couple of clerks to replace their clothes, torn in a tussle which they had had in his presence, and evidently for his amusement, at Tickhill. At the marriage of the first Edward's daughter Margaret, " the fool of the Count of Artois " occurs in company with such performers as Bastin Noblet of Liège, dancer, and Janyn le Get of Douai, minstrel ; and three years earlier in 1287, when the King entertained Alphonso of Aragon at Oleron, he presented a horse to the Spanish king's " woman fool and minstrel." Examples of female fools are rather rare, the most famous being Jane the Fool, who was a prominent member of the retinue of Henry VIII, and perhaps deserved the qualifying epithet less than those of her sex who were willing to become the bluff but fickle monarch's consorts. Outside the realm of mere folly, women entertainers were quite a common feature of medieval life, their usual performances being posturing and tumbling, especially balancing themselves on their hands, as early artists with singular unanimity show Herodias, or as a " little singing girl " did before Edward I at Breteuil. Amongst the minstrels to whom that same king gave money in the last year of his life was Maud Makejoye, who was a dancer, and no doubt deserved her nickname better than a contemporary William Makejoye, whose name has only survived through his being, most inappropriately, hanged for stealing. Several curious nicknames occur in this list of payments to minstrels, such as John du Chat, whether so called from the tone of his voice, for his power of imitating that vociferous but unmelodious beastie, or from the material of his viol strings (sheep-gut being more usual than cat-gut at that time and fox-gut being undesirable, according to one abnormally unveracious writer, because the vibrations of such strings would scare all the poultry within hearing). Others were " Gaunsaillie," whose name I cannot interpret, " Guille sanz manière," or " Unmannerly Will," Robert " le Boistous " or " the Boisterous " and, most pleasing of all, " Perle in the Eghe." Whether this last took his name from a perpetual dewy tear, or from some more solid pearl in his eye, deponent knoweth not ; but I picture him as a sad fellow, and a foil to his boisterous and unmannerly companions, whom I suspect to have been sad dogs—which is quite another sadness. King Edward's own royal band included two harpers—or possibly three, if " Jack " de Vesey's unnamed instrument was a harp—viols, two " Crouderes "—John and Tegwaret, the latter probably a Welshman, both from his name and from the " cruth " being a Welsh form of fiddle—

a tabourer and at least two " trompours," as might
be expected from so martial a king, for " in
bataylle the noyse of the trompe comfortyth
werryours, and the more stronge that the tromp-
ynge is the more stronge and bolde men ben to
fyghte." Possibly it was to encourage the martial
ardour of his sons that the king assigned five
trumpeters to the Prince of Wales and two to the
young Thomas of Brotherton. Besides his trumpeters the Prince had a " nakerer "—a player upon
those nakers or drums, which the musicians of the
" White Company " with such perverse ingenuity,
insisted upon blowing—Jakemin le Cateloyn, who
was " his Grace's own particular drum." Not
the least interesting people in this list of Edwardian
musicians are the five minstrel kings—" le Roy de
Champeigne, le Roy Capenny, le Roy Baisescu, le
Roy Marchis and le Roy Robert "—who seem to
have corresponded to the herald kings-at-arms,
Capenny being apparently king for Scotland. A
better-known minstrel king was the king of the
minstrels of Tutbury, whose regality was established by old John of Gaunt, and who bore sway
over the music makers of the Staffordshire honour,
held his court, feasted royally and set his subjects
to catch the greased bull, even down to the last
quarter of the prosaic eighteenth century.

If the Edwards and their successors kept up royal
orchestras, it is natural that Henry VIII should
do so. He was himself a composer of music, as
he was also a compounder of medicines, a writer
of ballads and theological treatises, an actor, a
bit of an architect and something of a costumier ;
but it was probably jealousy, rather than appreciation of Wolsey's private band, that caused him

to borrow the Cardinal's musicians and keep them hard at playing all night, which killed the excellent but unfortunate player upon that most exhausting instrument the shalme. Incidentally, Henry does not seem to have had a shalme player in his band, which, exclusive of trumpeters, consisted of a harper, two rebeks, three luters, two vialls—Hans Hyhorne and Hans Hosenet—six sagbuts, three minstrels, a tabret, two " dromslades " or drummers and, " as a tabour makyth the better melody yf there is a pype therwyth," a fyfer. Henry's daughter Mary not only spent much money in rewards to the minstrels and musicians of her father, brother and noble friends but, by her mother's advice, learnt to play both the virginals and the lute, Master Paston teaching her the former, and Philip van Wilder instructing her on the lute. For, although wandering musicians were regarded as idle vagabonds, music itself was recognised as a needful part of the education of a gentleman, and the young squires in the fifteenth century were expected to learn " sondry languages and othyr learninges vertuous, to harping, to pype, sing, daunce and with other honest and temperate behaviour and patience." And in the year that Mary ascended the throne we find Mr. Horseley teaching that important young gentleman Francis Willoughby " arethmetick and to playe on the virginalles " at 16d. the week, Rychards of Thaxsted also teaching him to play on the virginals and to sing, and a nameless person teaching him to dance. Part of the duties, also, of the Dean of the Royal Chapel was " to drawe these chyldren in songe, organes or suche other vertuous thinges," from which, incidentally, it may be noted that the organ was then, and always has been pre-eminently the virtuous instrument, and that employed in churches, though whether it is virtuous because it is always found in churches, or whether it is always found in churches because it is virtuous, is a nice question which may be debated by those who have nothing else to do. Suffice it that from the days of St. Jerome—when its bellows were made of the skins of elephants—onwards, the organ has been the church instrument. St. Dunstan, that cunning craftsman who caught the Devil by the nose, made an organ with bronze pipes for Malmesbury Abbey, which was still unrivalled 150 years later. At the close of the medieval period there was at Bordeaux " in the cathedrall church of seynt Andrews the fairist and the gretest payer of Orgyns in al Crystendome, in the whiche Orgins be many instrumentes and vyces as Giants heds and sterres, the whyche doth move and wagge with their jawes and eyes as fast as the player playeth."

But even this marvel of the sixteenth century is inferior, to my mind, to that organ of 400 pipes which good Bishop Elphage built for Winchester Cathedral in the tenth century, at the blowing of which seventy men laboured till the sweat poured off them, while its iron-tongued thunder roared forth with such a blast that it could be heard all over the ancient town of Winchester !

X. Tenures—Sporting and Sportive

" I HAVE gone rownde aboute Crystendome, and
overthwarte Crystendome, and a thousande
or two and more myles out of Crystendom, yet
there is not so moche pleasure for harte and
hynde, bucke and doo, and for roo bucke and doo
as in England." The truth of Borde's remark
will be the more readily admitted if we premise
that the pleasure is rather derived from the deer
than created for them. It is true that a northern
prelate has in this so-called twentieth century
publicly upheld foxhunting on the ground that the
foxes have a much happier life when preserved
than they would if treated as common vermin (no
doubt the Emperor Nero would have justified to
His Grace the use of Christians in the arenas on
similar grounds), but it may be doubted if the
medieval stag ever appreciated his privileged
position, remarkable as it was. For with all due
deference, and that is very little, to the country
magistrates who still consider that a rabbit has
more claims to the protection of the law than a
woman, it remains a remarkable fact that wild
animals should be preferred above human beings.
Yet so it was, and Norman William was neither
the first nor the last king to love the tall deer like
a father, though the imperial scale of his operations
in the formation of the New Forest,—exaggerated
by the ancient chroniclers with their usual reckless
disregard for exactitude,—has caught the popular
fancy and given him more than his share of sporting

Tenures—Sporting and Sportive

fame. From the days when Guinevere watched King Arthur chase the white stag with his good hound Cavall, whose footprint endured a thousand years on the mountains of Builth, and, for all I know, is still there, hunting has been the pursuit of the great ones of this land. Kings and nobles and lesser lords rivalled one another in upholding the sanctity of beasts of the chase, and medieval England was full of mutilated men who had been guilty of aping their betters in indulging an appetite for venison and sport with the added excitement of illegality, while jails, both medieval and modern, must have been unpleasantly crowded with lesser offenders who had incurred suspicion, not always unjustly, by the possession of relics of rabbits or greater game, or by wandering in the forests with bows and arrows or dogs. Nor did it require overcrowding to make some of these prisons places not merely of passive detention but of actual pain and punishment. The forest prison that Peter de Neville built at Allexton in Rutland during the lawless years which followed the Barons' War, unlike his title to possess a private jail, not only would but did hold water, and unfortunate men such as Peter son of Constantine, who was arrested " on suspicion of a rabbit," might lie in the water if they would not or could not find two pence for the privilege of sitting on a bench. The forest bailiwick of this same Peter de Neville had a curious origin, for it was said that when Henry I, as keen a sportsman as his father and brother, was riding through the forest he saw five hinds together in one place, and at once detached one of his followers to watch the place and keep the five hinds till his return. He never did return, but, as the Russian sentry posted by Great Catherine to keep unpicked the first snowdrop of the year patrolled the palace lawn for a century after the snowdrop and the empress both were dead, so the place where once the five hinds had been was still watched over when the third Henry was tottering to his grave.

With their predominant interest in sport it was natural enough that our early kings, when they granted lands for a nominal rent, should often exact, in lieu of the lawyer's peppercorn or clove gilly-flower, some hunting weapon, and the exchequer must have been cluttered up with boar-spears, bows, and, above all, arrows. Arrows singly, or by twos or threes, or by the score,—barbed arrows, great broad arrows, heavy enough to " draw blood from a weather-cock," arrows fletched with feathers of the grey goose, arrows, three in number and sent up from Doddinghurst in Essex, fletched with eagle's feathers and bound with gold thread, arrows so numerous that even the industrious and sonorous antiquary, Hercules Malebysse Beckwith, did not trouble to record them. With the Doddinghurst arrows might be classed the three arrows feathered of peacocks which the tenant of Lympstone had to present, stuck into an oaten loaf worth half a farthing, when the King came to hunt on Dartmoor. But as a matter of fact peacock-feathered arrows were neither merely ornamental nor reserved to royalty, and Chaucer's Knight's yeoman bore " A shefe of peacock arwes bright and kene." As to the accompanying loaf, it was a small but doubtless welcome contribution to the lunch of the royal hunter, who, however, fared better when he hunted on Exmoor, as then he received from a tenement in Barnstaple not only three barbed arrows, but also a salmon. Food renders were common enough, and a penurious king might have kept himself and his family, if not his household, on these rents in kind, and not had reason to complain of lack of variety in the menu. There were lampreys from the Severn, eels from a score of places, cheeses and pears from la Réole, pearmains from Norfolk, though the Lord Treasurer intercepted these and sent them off to his wife, and a gallon of honey from the unromantic neighbourhood of Newington Butts, paid by the Queen's goldsmith, and doubtless consumed by his royal mistress in her parlour while her husband was counting out his money. Several estates supplied wine, one sent perry, and another, in Somerset, home-made clove wine, warming and good for the digestion. No fewer than three townships were concerned in supplying the King with herring pies ; Yarmouth provided a hundred herrings of the first catch of the season, Norwich made them into twenty-four pies with pepper and ginger, galingale and other strange and savoury spices, and the lord of East Carleton carried them to the King, receiving on his arrival at the court a good square meal for his trouble. Besides the supplying of food, there were other tenures connected with the kitchen, lands being held by such services as providing withies with which to hang up meat in the King's kitchen (this, suitably enough, at Hungerford), supplying the King with hot rolls daily, dressing his pot herbs, or scalding his hogs. After the food had been obtained and cooked yet other lands were involved in the serving of it. Not only were there the

famous service privileges connected with corona-
tions, which are too well known to need quoting,
and the hereditary offices of royal butler, server,
pantler, and so forth, but the great lords, clerical
and lay, exacted similar services. The Abbot of
Battle granted lands in Sussex to be held by the
service of acting as his cup-bearer when he attended
Parliament ; Henry le Forcer held his lands by
acting as butler and pantler to the Harcourts for
forty days, and carving for the Prior of Wenlock
on St. Milberge's day, as Ela, Countess of Warwick,
for her manor of Hook Norton, had to carve for
Edward I on Christmas Day ; and carving was no
light task, but a fine art, and the Countess might
well have felt flustered at being called upon to
" breke that dere, lesche that brawne, rere that
goose, lyft that swanne, sauce that capon, spoyle
that henne, frusshe that chekyn, unlace that cony,
dysmembre that heron, dysfygure that pecocke
alaye that fesande, wynge that partryche," and
perform other similar feats in the correct manner.
Presumably she employed some expert deputy,
but the head of the ancient and noble house of
Willoughby of Eresby had in his own person, or
in that of his eldest son, to act as waiter, and carry
dishes to the table of the Bishop of Durham at his
consecration and at Christmas and Whitsun, while
the still more ancient and semi-royal house of
Courtenay of Devon performed a similar service
at the consecration of the Bishops of Exeter.
For the Yorkshire manor of Levington the first
of the Louvaine Percies had to go on Christmas
day to Skelton Castle, attend the lady of the Castle,
his mother-in-law, to Mass in the chapel, and afterwards dine with her. But was this a service or a

Tenures—Sporting and Sportive

privilege ? As the much-bored bishop replied when asked if he did not see the hand of Providence in the preservation, narrated at great length, of his prosy companion's aunt : " Not knowing the lady, I cannot say."

Returning to the subject of food : there were many estates whose tenants had to provide refreshment for their overlord if he should happen to come to the neighbourhood. Sometimes the obligation took the form of entertainment for the night, or of a good meal for the lord and all his attendants, but often it was a smaller render of more definite character. The lord of Winterslow had to make claret-cup for the King when he came to Clarendon, and the tenant of lands in West Sussex had to present the King with two white capons if he passed his gate, while Blount records a curious tenure by which, if the King crossed Shrivenham Bridge, a neighbouring landowner brought to him two white capons, saying, " Behold, my lord, these two white capons which you shall have another time but not now." This is one of those strange jocular tenures whose origin is as tantalisingly withheld from us as were the capons from the King ; and another, mentioned in the same book and said to have been performed as late as 1680, was that connected with Essington. The lord of this manor, or his deputy, had to come on New Year's Day to Hilton and drive a goose three times round the fire in the hall (from which it would seem, incidentally, that they still had a central fire in Hilton Hall as late as 1680), while Jack of Hilton, a little brass figure filled with water which produced a whistling noise under the influence of the heat, was blowing the fire. Geese figured also at Aylesbury, where one would have expected ducks, two being given to the King if he came there in the summer, or three eels if he came in the winter, the tenants also providing litter for his bed and rushes or straw to carpet his bed-chamber.[1] Litter for the royal bed was also provided at Brockenhurst when the King hunted in the New Forest, while if he preferred to hunt in the Oxfordshire forest of Witchwood he was assured of a more substantial meal than the vanishing capons of Shrivenham, as one of his tenants was bound to bring him a roast of pork, and it was presumably to remove the traces of this substantial but greasy fare that another tenant had to bring a towel to wipe the King's hands. It is not improbable that occasionally the provision of the roast of pork was bringing coals to New-castle, for kings and lesser sportsmen appreciated the chase of the wild boar, and Witchwood was one of the places where they indulged therein. And a fine sport it was, with more than a slight spice of danger. Twrch Trwyth with his seven pigs defied King Arthur and the champions of Britain, slew Arthur's two uncles and his chief architect, Gwilenhin King of France, Hirpeissawg King of Armorica, and many score others, laid waste a fifth part of Ireland, and ravaged Wales and Cornwall before he was driven into the sea. The Brawn of Brauncepeth was a poor thing beside Twrch Trwyth, yet he did some killing in his day, and even the ordinary nameless wild boar of the forest could " slytte a man fro the knee up to the brest and slee hym al starke dede at one stroke."

[1] The tenant of Stow in Cambridgeshire provided hay for the purpose for which Gargantua commended a goose's neck.

Although the wild boar afforded such fine sport, the evidence seems to point to its having been less frequently hunted for amusement in this country in early times than killed for food. For the matter of that, even deer were looked on in a much more utilitarian light than the modern advocates of sport for sport's sake would care to admit ; and although it was true that " great men do not set so moch by the meate as they do by the pastyme of kyllyng of it," it is equally true that the packs of royal hounds and huntsmen were largely employed in keeping the King's larder well stocked with venison. " And although the flesshe be dispraysed in physycke," said one who was himself a doctor, and a clever one at that, " I pray God to sende me parte of the flesshe to eate, physycke notwithstandyng. . . . I am sure it is a lordes dysshe, and I am sure it is good for an Englysshe man, for it doth anymate hym to be as he is, whiche is, strong and hardy." Venison might be termed the meat of the extremes, being in theory reserved to the great and, in a way, to the poorest and most wretched of men,—in practice it was, of course, eaten by many who belonged to neither class, but who ran considerable risk of being reduced to poverty and misery if caught with telltale bones, ears, or antlers in their possession ; and while " venesoun with frumenty " might be a dish for a lord, it must be admitted that the physicians were justified in looking askance at the venison, in the shape of the bodies of deer found dead in the forests, which was given to the infirm paupers of the hospitals. Such gifts are often recorded on the forest rolls, and it is rather noteworthy that one, Walter Barun, who held land in

Somerset by hanging up on a wooden gallows the
deer found dead of murrain on Exmoor, had also
to entertain the sick poor who came to him, at his
own cost : if we are correct in inferring that he
set off the two services against one another by
feeding the beggars on the deer, it is probable that
their sickness was emphasised and their number
diminished. One instance in which the poor of
Rockingham benefited in this way occurred in
1246, when they received the body of a mad hind
that was seen stumbling and falling about in the
forest for some time before it died. It is surely
more than a coincidence that on the very day on
which the hind lost its reason and its life, a tremendous duel between two harts was witnessed in the
neighbouring park of Brigstock, resulting in the
death of one of the combatants. The connection
between the two events is so obvious that we are
justified in attributing the hind's insanity and
death to "an affair of the heart," especially as a
pun—for I will neither pretend that the play upon
words was accidental, nor attempt to evade responsibility by the use of the blessed word paronomasia
—was a medieval weakness quite appropriate to
the date of the story. John de Warenne, Earl of
Surrey, just thirty years later, claimed sporting
rights all over his vast estates on the ground that
when his ancestors lost their Norman estates King
John, to recompense them, gave them universal
rights of warren "for the sake of their name."

Warrens and madness alike suggest that "good
lytyl beest" the hare, in the hunting of whom is
"much good sport and lykyng." Coursing the
hare was a very favourite sport in early days ;
and about the time that the Earl of Surrey and

Tenures—Sporting and Sportive

Peter of Savoy were trying, with considerable success, to appropriate all the sporting rights in East Sussex and were bullying such of their unfortunate tenants as dared attempt to preserve their crops from the inroads of the game, a West Sussex gentleman with the not unsuitable name of Covert established the right of himself and his co-tenants to hunt hares in the woods of Bramber Rape on Shrove Tuesday, and to cut bats to throw at them. The selection of Shrove Tuesday might suggest that the hares were destined to provide the last meat feast of the season before Lent set in ; but, apart from the fact that the hares would have been better for keeping, their flesh was not greatly in demand, and indeed it was considered better " for the houndes or dogges to eate the hare after they have kylled it than man shuld eate it, for it is not praysed, nother in the Olde Testament nother in physycke ; for the byble sayth the hare is an unclene beeste, and physycke sayeth hares flesshe is drye and doth ingender melancholy humors." Still, provided her flesh were not eaten—or at least only her brains, which were held as good to strengthen the memory as her blood to remove freckles,—she " doth no harme nor dyspleasure to no man." Therein, it need hardly be pointed out, the hare differs from the wolf and the fox. So far as wolves are concerned, they were regarded frankly as vermin to be destroyed ; and although the popular tradition of their extinction under King Edgar is wrong by about six centuries, they had become distinctly rare in England by the beginning of the thirteenth century, and towards the end of that century, when Richard de Loveraz was recorded to hold his land by the service of hunting the wolf in Hampshire, it was added " if one can be found." The same qualification was added at a later date in the case of Alan de Wulf-hunte, whose duty it was to drive wolves out of Sherwood Forest. The family of Engayne held lands in Northants by chasing the wolf through four counties, and other lands in Huntingdonshire by chasing wolf, fox, hare, and cat. Here, as in many other cases, the fox is named as vermin to be destroyed, and so he was regarded for the most part until a comparatively late date. To the medieval sportsman the fox was of little account, and almost the only thing to be said in favour of hunting him was that he was easy to follow, as " he stinketh evermore as he flieth," against which veracious but unflattering comment on the chartered libertine of the modern countryside may be set the complaint of the old huntsman that the scent had been spoilt by " them nasty stinking voilets." With the harmless hare, the odoriferous fox, and the evasive wolf, was classed the wild cat—and this creature, now as extinct as the wolf in England, was perhaps the most fierce and savage of our native wild beasts, for though there was more danger in the wild boar's tusk, or in the fangs of the ravening wolf, empoisoned by its diet of toads, yet " if any beest hath the develis streynt in hym without doute it is the catt, and that both the wilde and the tame."

If there were many estates held by the service, or with the privilege, of killing cats and other vermin, there were also many for which the tenants had to take charge of their lord's hunting-dogs. Sometimes several hounds, or even a whole pack, had to be maintained, but more usually the responsibility was limited to a single hound which had to be kept or trained, and that the latter process was not " all done by kindness " may be guessed from the fact that I have found a tenure, usually described as " by nourishing (*nutriciendi*) " a dog, entered on one occasion as " by whipping (*castigandi*) " a dog,—a distinction in terminology which probably did not make much difference in practice. More humane, or at least more in accordance with modern sentiment, was the serjeantry of Purse Caundel, by which the Fitz Alans had to look after any of the King's hounds that were injured while he was hunting on Blackmoor—by no means a sinecure, for a stag at bay would play havoc with his pursuers, and Turberville tells of a boar which left but twelve out of a pack of fifty hounds unscathed. For the most part the canine serjeantries are of little interest except for their specification of the various types of sporting dogs, of which the most curious was a white brach with red ears, like the hounds of King Arawn of Annwn, whose " hair was of a brilliant shining white, and their ears were red ; and as the whiteness of their bodies shone, so did the redness of their ears glisten." With the exception of this picturesque piebald brach the colour scheme of the hounds seems to have been left to the choice of the tenant, but the kind of dog, most frequently a greyhound, was naturally specified, as otherwise the King might have been put off with anything, from the " smalle ladye's popees that bere awaye the flees " to the witless alaunt. These great alaunts and mastiffs, strong, savage, and stupid, were used for hunting the wild boar, and were also kept in large numbers as house dogs, in which

capacity they occasionally contributed to their
master's larder by pulling down a deer. To check
this tendency all mastiffs kept in the forest districts had to have the three toes of their forefeet
cut off, and in order to see that this was duly done
the Somerset foresters adopted the ingenious but
provocative method of marching through the
villages blowing their horns and making so much
noise that all the mastiffs rushed out and barked
furiously at them. The trick was effective, but
did not tend to the popularity of the foresters.

Horns have been associated with hunting from
the earliest times, and many hunting treatises
contain elaborate descriptions not only of the
various calls to be blown upon them, but also of
the size and materials of which they should be
constructed for the varying rank of their users ;
and a medieval hunt must have been a noisy affair
with all the beaters, huntsmen, and foresters
sounding their horns and cheering on the hounds.
Oddly enough, hunting-horns do not seem to figure
among the miscellaneous assortment of articles,
ranging from gilt spurs to garlands of roses, paid
by way of rent, but there were a number of cases
in which the blowing of a horn[1] formed part of
the annual service exacted, and several others in
which a particular horn constituted the charter or
title-deed by which the estate was held. At
Bradford in Yorkshire, Northop of Manningham
held certain lands by coming into the market-place
on Martinmas with a horn, a halbert, and a hound,

---

[1] A blast of a different kind had to be sounded for certain
lands in Suffolk, whose tenant had to come to Court at Christmas, and " faire un saut un siffle et un pet " at one and the
same time.

and blowing three blasts on his horn ; finding some difficulty in manipulating the halbert, the horn, and the hound at the same time, one of the family gave a piece of land to Rushworth of Horton on condition that he should hold the hound while he sounded his horn. In Chingford there was an estate held of the rector, of which, whenever it changed hands the new owner with his wife (I presume that, as in the case of the Hampshire wolf, we may add " if there be one "), his man servant, and his maid, each mounted on a horse, had to come to the rectory, the owner carrying a hawk and his servant leading a grey-hound. On arriving, instead of ringing the bell, the new tenant blew three blasts on his horn ; they then all dined with the rector, who had the use of the hawk and the hound for the day, but had to provide a chicken for the hawk and a loaf of bread for the hound, and after dinner another three blasts were blown and the visitors went home. This was still done in the eighteenth century, but if it has been kept up till the present day, I should be glad to know whether it is more difficult to find a rector who can fly a hawk, or a maid-servant who can ride a horse. Of the charter horns which still exist, the most famous is the horn of Ulphus, or Ulf ; by it the Saxon thane Ulf bestowed his lands upon the minster of York, and in the minster treasury it remained until the spoliative days of Edward VI, when it disappeared, afterwards falling into the hands of that learned antiquary and gallant soldier, Lord Fairfax, the most attractive of all the Parliamentarian leaders, whose son restored it to the minster. Several others exist, including the Pusey horn, by which, according to tradition and its inscription, King Canute gave Pusey to William Pewse, who apparently had the remarkable forethought to adopt a surname some three generations before the use of such valuable aids to identification had been assumed by any persons except the equally legendary founders of other ancient families. It was at Pusey, centuries before the name became associated with Catholic revivals, that a family called Paternoster held land by saying a paternoster daily for the souls of the King's ancestors ; and Richard Paternoster, on the death of his brother, duly appeared at the Exchequer and paid his death and succession duties to the Barons by reciting three paternosters and three aves : this tenure is presumably extinct, but if not it is probable that the succeeding tenant at the present day would have to throw in a credo or the ten commandments by way of super-tax. There was land in Buxted held of the Archbishop of Canterbury by similar service of a daily prayer, and in Leicestershire there was an estate held by saying paternoster and ave five times daily for the soul of King John, who certainly required them as much as anybody. Another curious service was the obligation of William de Valoignes, in the event of the King coming to his Kentish manor of Mappiscombe and going to hear Mass, to provide his royal guest with a penny for the offertory. Still more curious was the custom by which on Palm Sunday the representative of the lord of the manor of Broughton came to Castor Church with a new cart-whip, which he cracked three times in the church porch ; he then took his seat in the manor pew, but came out at the beginning of the second lesson and knelt in front of the reading-desk, holding over the parson's head a purse, containing thirty silver pennies, tied on the end of the whip-lash.

We have wandered somewhat, from the forest to the church, but we can return by way of St. Paul's. For some three hundred years or more, on the 29th of June, a fat buck was brought up from Essex to the cathedral, where its body was received at the choir steps by the canons in full vestments, wearing chaplets of flowers, and the horns of the buck were then carried on a spear in procession through the church with a musical accompaniment of horn-blowing. Rather similar, but even gayer, was the scene in Tutbury Church on the Assumption of the Blessed Virgin. On that day (15th August) a buck was presented to the Prior of Tutbury ; its head " cabaged," or as the modern heralds say, " caboshed "—that is to say, cut off close behind the ears—and " garnished aboute with a rye of pease," was carried by the keeper in whose ward it had been killed. In his company came all the other keepers, riding two and two, and carrying green boughs in their hands, and in front of them went all the minstrels of the honour, two and two, while the rear of the procession was brought up by the wood-master or his deputy. At the town cross the keepers blew a " seeke " in chorus, and a little farther on they halted again and blew a " recheate "—the call by which hounds are brought back from a false scent. On reaching the churchyard the procession halted and dismounted and entered the church, all the minstrels playing on their instruments " during the offeringe tyme," and the wood-master offered up the buck's head, or rather, as it would seem from the wording of the record, a silver model of it, the keepers each giving a penny at the same time. As soon as the buck's head had been offered all the keepers blew a " morte " three times, and at once adjourned to a chapel, where they heard Mass, after which they marched up to the castle and had dinner at the Prior's expense.

Tutbury was associated with quite a number of curious customs, amongst which may be counted the services due from the lord of Tattenhill. Sir Philip Somerville, whom I should like to connect with William Somerville, the poet of " The Chase," had to come to Tutbury on Lammas Day (the 1st of August) and announce his willingness to hunt venison for his lord's larder. The steward then provided a horse and saddle, worth 50s., and a " bercelett " hound for Sir Philip's use, and had, further, to pay him daily for the six weeks during which his service lasted, two shillings and sixpence for himself and a shilling for his servant and his hound. The parkers and foresters were then summoned and put at his disposal, and he remained in control of the hunt until Holy Rood Day (14th September), when " the sayd Sir Phelippe shall returne to the Castle of Tuttebury, upon the sayd horse with his bercelett, and shal dyne with the steward or receyver ; and after dynner he shall deliver the horse, sadyle, and bercelett to the steward or receyvour and shal kisse the porter and depart." Whether Sir Philip or the porter would be the more embarrassed by the affectionate leave-taking may be open to question, but it perhaps assisted matters, if indeed it had not originated the custom, that the chaste salute was given after

dinner. This same Sir Philip was also lord of
Whichnor, where he had to keep a "flyke of
bacon" hanging in his hall, to be given on the
same conditions as the more famous Dunmow
flitch. When a claim was made for the bacon a
day was appointed, on which Knyghtley of Rudlowe and all others who "owe services to the
Baconne" attended at the manor gate at sunrise
and waited for the claimant, who was led "wythe
tromps and tabours and other manner of myn-
stralseye" to the hall door, where the flitch was
lying on a sack of wheat and a sack of rye. There
the claimant knelt, and with his hand on a book
resting upon the flitch made oath as follows :
"Here ye, Sir Philip de Somervyle, lord of Whiche-
noure, mayntayner and giver of this baconne, that
I, A, syth I wedded B, my wife, and syth I had
her in my kepyng and at my wylle by a yere and
a daye after our marryage, I wold not have
chaunged for none other, farer ne fowler, richer
ne powrer, ne for none other descended of gretter
lynage, slepyng ne wakyng, at noo tyme. And if
the said B were sole and I sole, I wolde take her
to be my wife before all the wymen of the worlde,
of what conditions soevere they be, good or evyle ;
as helpe me God and His seyntys and this flesh
and all fleshes." Two neighbours had then to
swear that they believed this to be true, and the
flitch was delivered to him, with half a quarter of
wheat and a cheese if he were a freeman, or half
a quarter of rye and no cheese if he were a villein.
Then Knyghtley of Rudlowe put the corn and
bacon on his horse and the successful claimant
mounted his own horse, or one lent him by Sir
Philip, with the cheese in front of him, "and soe

shall they departe the manoyr of Whichenour with the corne and the baconne to fore hym that hath wonne ytt, with trompets, tabourets, and other manoir of mynstralce.''

XI. Some Strange Tales ◦ ◦ ◦

" IN this same year the Justices in eyre at York
acted right sternly, and a certain nobleman,
Simon le Constable, who was arrested for many
felonies, did they put to the penalty of the law
because he refused to abide the verdict of a jury.
And he died in prison." So writes the annalist
of Dunstable Priory under the year 1293, evidently
with a feeling that the severity of the Justices
towards a member of a county family was a thing
to be remarked upon and even deprecated. The
story that lies behind this may tend to reconcile
us to the fate of the noble Simon and seems to me,
in any case, worth telling, as affording some
insight into the less reputable side of the life of a
medieval baron. This Simon was head of the
great family of Constable of Halsham—not to be
confounded with the Constables of Flamborough,
who claimed kinship, on the spindle-side, with
John of the One Eye and his more famous son,
Eustace, victim of one of the unfortunate incidents
of the Welsh expedition of 1157. One of Simon's
neighbours, Sir John de Danthorpe, had married
Katherine, daughter of Philip de Weelsby, whose
fascinations proved too much for Simon, himself
a married man. Accordingly he carried off the
fair Katherine, and, which was possibly the greater
source of annoyance to her husband, her goods.
Such a scandal could hardly be allowed to pass
unrebuked, and the Archbishop dropped on him
and brought pressure to bear so effectually that

he confessed his sin and promised amendment.
Upon his expressing contrition he was pardoned,
on condition that he should go, in person or by
a deputy who should be "a first-class fighting
man" (*ydoneum bellatorem*), to the Holy Land;
a further condition being that if he offended again
with Katherine he should pay £100 towards the
Crusade fund. This was in 1275, and possibly he
went on crusade, but if he did he was not cured
of his infatuation, for five years later the lovers
were excommunicated by bell and candle throughout the Deanery of Holderness for their contumacy.
About this time Sir John de Danthorpe died,
possibly with a little assistance from Sir Simon,
who further simplified matters by poisoning his
own wife, Joan. Archbishop Wickwane had
ordered his official to proceed against Katherine,
but in November, 1281, directed him to suspend
action, out of regard for the reputation of "that
knight of whom you know," of whose reformation
he had, or professed to have, hope. The next
move was that Simon married Katherine much to
the annoyance of the Archbishop, who had reluc-
tantly to admit that the marriage was legal.
Although the facts of the case must have been
pretty notorious, there is nothing to show that
Sir Simon was thought any the worse of, or that
his neighbours refused to call on Katherine; in
fact, everything points to their ten years of married
life having passed quite normally. During this
time Simon is constantly found acting in a magis-
terial capacity, being, for instance, appointed with
one John Sampson in 1286 to inquire as to the
vagabonds in the city of York who committed so
many murders and robberies that men dared not

go out of their houses without armed escort. But at last the blow fell, and in 1293 the Justices came down into Yorkshire to hold assizes, and, as we have said, " acted right sternly." A long list of offences they had to try, and amongst the offenders was Sir Simon le Constable, charged on two counts, if not more. One charge was that he had carried off twelve oxen belonging to the Prioress of Swine, and had stocked his larder therewith ; the other that he had abducted Katherine, wife of Sir John de Danthorpe, and her goods, against her husband's will. Against Katherine herself was brought the charge that she had poisoned her husband, and Sir Simon's first wife and also one Henry de Thorley, by the aid of Beatrice de Ver, Joan Constable's maid. Beatrice had been convicted and burnt for her share in the crime, and it would seem that Sir Simon had tried to shield himself by putting the blame on to Katherine. If so, he was unsuccessful, as the twelve jurors were unanimous in declaring her innocent, the least positive of them, Hugh de Karlo, being content to say that he didn't think she had done it, while Sir Robert de Stuteville and four other knights asserted her innocence on their conscience and by the common report of the country ; Thomas de Poynton agreed with them because he had never heard any suggestion against her except by Robert Constable, son of the murdered Joan, and by Roger Lascelles, whose daughter Robert had married. Stephen de Thorp pointed out that Katherine was not in the house when Joan was poisoned (the question of her own husband appears to have been dropped) and Hugh de Pokelynton supplied the information that she was at the time in Norfolk, taking seisin of the manor of Wenys, which Simon had given her, and added that after her marriage she hated Beatrice de Ver, whom she found living in the house, and turned her out and would not let her stay, because of her infamous act—from which it would seem, incidentally, that the murder was no secret. Two other jurors acquitted her on the ground that Beatrice after her conviction admitted her own guilt but expressly declared Katherine innocent, and Sir Nicholas de Leycestre exposed the whole conspiracy by saying that some time earlier he was on a jury before which Sir Simon was accused of the crime, and many of his friends brought pressure to bear that the crime should be put upon Katherine, that so Sir Simon should be saved. The lady was therefore acquitted, and her husband charged with the murder, but he, seeing that conviction was certain, refused to plead, and the Justices, being unable to compel him to stand his trial, inflicted the penalty of the law, the *peine forte et dure*. This was, to blend terms borrowed from the Suffragettes and the Trades Unions, a " hunger lock-out "; the recalcitrant prisoner being thrown into the worst prison and given only a little water one day and a little bread the next. Under this treatment Sir Simon le Constable died before the assizes were ended, but we may afford him a little admiration for the courage with which he endured forcible starving, for thereby he saved his lands from escheating, as they would have done if he had been condemned as a convicted felon, and they therefore descended intact to his son, though his chattels were forfeited, and as some proof of his wealth it may be mentioned that these chattels on his Yorkshire estates alone were valued at over £366.

It would be an exaggeration to say that Sir Simon was a typical baron of his day, but not a very gross exaggeration. At these same assizes Jordan le Vavassour, a member of another leading Yorkshire family, was hanged for killing his wife's sister in order to get her lands, and, so far as poisoning is concerned, it was in the next year that Master Wynand de Bryland, rector of Snodland, in Kent, dined with Solomon of Rochester, one of the best known, not to say most notorious, judges of the King's Bench, and took the opportunity to poison his host. The rector had probably acted at the instigation of the Bishop of Rochester ; at any rate, when he claimed benefit of clergy the court took the unusual course of refusing to hand him over to his own ordinary, the Bishop of Rochester, on the ground that he was *familiaris et collateralis* of the bishop, who had, moreover, stated his intention of acquitting him, both before and after his civil trial ; he was, therefore, handed over to Canterbury, but some months later the king allowed Rochester to have him, and he promptly went through the farce of purgation and recovered his liberty.

From poisoning to sorcery is no great step, and if the clergy occasionally dealt in deadly drugs it is not surprising that they should sometimes have dealings with those evil spirits against whom they were supposed to defend their flocks. One of the most curious cases of sorcery on record, which occurred in Yorkshire the year that Henry VIII, of dread memory, ascended the throne, began through John Wilkinson, canon of Drax, and vicar

of Bingley, telling the vicar of Addingham that
"there was as moche goolde in a place besides
Halifax as wold raunsome a king; and that oone
Leventhorp, nowe dede, had seene the foote of
the kist, and the devell sitting upon it, and that
he put a swerd to remove it, and he nypped it a
soundre in the myddist, as it had been a rish;
and the said Sir John saide it cold never be gott
but with losse of a Cristen sole." His chaplain,
Richard Grenewood, confirmed his story, and said
that they had been to the spot with John Stewerd,
a schoolmaster at Knaresborough, who rather
fancied himself as a wizard, and was reputed to
have three humble bees, which he kept " under a
stone in the erth and called theyme oute by oone
and oone and gave iche oone of theyme a drop of
blode of his fyngor." The priests, however, did
not think much of Stewerd, and after testing him
decided that " he could nought do, he was not so
connyng as they were." Stewerd himself, indeed,
under examination, admitted that he was a fraud,
and that " whenne personnes and people came to
him to have knowledge of thinges lost and stollen
he wold shewe theym a booke of astronomy and
made theyme beleve that he was connyng, and he
coulde no thing do, but some tyme it hapened as
he said, and that was as the blynde man cast his
staff"; from which it would seem that he resembled
the " gentylwoman, doughter unto the lorde of
Dyguon of the castell of Bethune, the which was
so lerned in astronomy that she toke upon her to
shewe thynges to come, wherin somtyme she
happed upon the soth, but more oftener she
fayled." Anyhow, Stewerd told the story of the
treasure to another priest, James Richardson, who

had come to him at the request of Thomas Jameson, ex-mayor of York, to inquire about a servant who had gone off with some goods. Then the three priests, the schoolmaster, the ex-mayor and two or three friends agreed to have a shot at getting the treasure. Accordingly Canon John brought his books from Drax Priory, and with their aid Richardson made a square " lamina " of lead and engraved on it four names, of which Storax was one, and the figure of the demon Oberion, in whom I suppose we may recognise Shakespeare's Oberon and the " wycckyd spyryte the whyche was callyd Oberycom," whose invocation caused a certain Londoner to be pilloried in 1444. The canon and Richardson, with the help of Jameson, next made a great circle of virgin parchment with all the due invocations and prayers, while Stewerd saw to the gilding of the sceptre or magic wand. All being ready, they set out for Mixendale, where the hoard lay (and, for all I know, still lies), but to avoid suspicion they went in three separate parties, Sir Richard Grenewood and a friend feigning to " go to gadir to Sir Richarde's fader's to eyte a henne," all to meet after dark at a certain cross on Wilston Lee moor. They carried with them, besides their magical apparatus, a number of " singing breads," or unconsecrated wafers, one of which Canon John was prepared to consecrate if the spirit were disobedient " and thenne the sprite shuld appere to hyme like a child of ij yere olde and thenne he wold obey." Unfortunately a heavy mist came on, and after wandering about on the moor they lost their way, and had to abandon the enterprise ; but they agreed to meet again in Arden Wood, as the canon, who was to

do the invocation, said it would be just as easy
to make " the sprite called Belphares " (possibly
a relation of Belphegor, Satanic ambassador to
France) carry the treasure to one place as another.
But on the appointed day Canon John failed to
turn up, and Jameson started quarrelling with the
rest of the company over the division of the gold
and the possession of the " sword of maytenaunce,"
which, with a book covered in black leather, lay
on top of the chest of gold, and it would seem that
in anger at their refusal to allow him the lion's
share of the phantom gold, the ex-mayor gave the
whole show away, though by so doing he involved
himself with his associates in the humiliation of a
public penance.

In the year that Thomas Jameson, who figures
in the last story, died, which was 1527, John
Curson of Kettering told some friends that there
were three thousand pounds in gold and silver
buried in two pots in a bank, possibly a tumulus,
beside Kettering cross. So they went to the place
and he pointed out the exact location of the
treasure, saying, " here standes the on pott within
the ground and here standes the other," adding
that he had got the information from a learned
man at the cost of twenty nobles. He further
said that he came once before with two men to
dig, but " when they hadde putt in a wymble
they heard such a lumbring within the ground
that they dyrst nott tarry with hym. And he
said that a man sprite and a woman sprite dyd
kepe the said ij pottes." Instead of the timid
men Curson this time " hadd his boo (boy) and
braught with hym ij pickaxes and a spade and a
spytt for to digg the same ground," but the

sprites were too clever for him, and nothing was found.

If priests, as we have said, sometimes dabbled in the black arts, women were notoriously addicted thereto, and although in early times witches were not such common objects of the countryside as they became, to their sorrow, in the sixteenth and following centuries, yet there must have been quite a sufficient supply at all times. Many of them were, no doubt, harmless enough unless provoked, but there was a strange case in Northumberland early in the reign of Edward I, when a witch came into the house of John de Kerneslawe at eve and flew at him because he made the sign of the cross over the lights when *Benedicite* was said. John, " defending himself as if from the devil," struck the witch with a knife and slew her. He promptly went off his head and became mad. By judgment of the clergy of the district the body of the witch was burnt, and John, recovering his wits and fearing to be arrested for the murder, fled, but was allowed to return as his act was held to be justified. The witch in this case was " an unknown woman," but in a certain number of instances the accused was far from unknown. One of the earliest and the most famous of all such cases was the trial of the wealthy, and much married, Irish lady, Dame Alice Kyteler in 1324. Her sacrifice of nine red cocks at the crossways shows that her methods were of respectable, pagan antiquity, and were worthy of a more impressive devil than " Robin MacCarthy " (so, at least, I read *filius Artis*), " one of the inferior spirits of hell " (*ex pauperioribus inferni*), while the *Grimoires* contain no ointment much more unpleasant than that which she compounded from the insides of the cocks mixed with spiders, " black insects like scorpions," and other horrid worms and herbs, with the brain of an unbaptised child, all boiled together in the skull of a thief. Of still greater position than Dame Alice was Jacquette, Duchess of Bedford, who was accused of having inveigled Edward IV into marriage with her daughter by witchcraft, on the evidence chiefly of " an image of lede made lyke a man of armes, conteynyng the length of a manne's fynger, and broken in the myddes "—in other words, a broken lead soldier. In the previous reign, in 1441, the Duchess of Gloucester was arrested for having plotted to slay the king " by crafte of egremauncey." Of her accomplices Roger Bolingbroke, " a man expert in nygromancy," and Margery Jourdemayne, the witch of Eye, who had been up before the Privy Council on a charge of sorcery in 1432, were executed, Master Thomas Southwell, rector of St. Stephen's, Walbrook, died in the Tower from terror, and the Duchess herself, after a penitential walk down Fleet Street with a taper in her hand, was banished to the Isle of Man.

The royal Henries appear to have been the mark of sorcerers. Queen Joan of Navarre was shut up in the marshland fortress of Pevensey for having practised witchcraft against Henry V, and a combination of sorcery and poisoning formed part of at least one plot against Henry IV. It was shortly after the first of the Lancastrian kings had seized the throne that Thomas Sandford, servant of John Inglewode, clerk, was sent down to Rye to John Salerne with letters from Robert Marner, canon of Ipswich, to be conveyed to Sluys.

In Salerne's house he met a merchant named Bernard, who lived near Shoreham, and who gave him a message to the effect that he could arrange for five hundred Flemish men-at-arms to come over. Not long afterwards Inglewode and the canon went down to Rye and paid Salerne £100, —which he said would cost him £1,000 and his life if the business did not go well ; then they rode back to London and met a Dominican friar, late confessor to King Richard, and held a long consultation over the tomb of Gilbert Beket, the father of the sainted Thomas, in " le pardonchirchehawe de Seynt Poules," and agreed to meet again at Langley. Sandford was then let into the secret of the plot, and told that if he were loyal it should prove greatly to his advantage, while Salerne for his share was to have the castle of Lewes and the constableship of Pevensey for life. The conspirators met as arranged at Langley and went on to Berkhampstead, where they put up at " Assherugge In," and there laid plans to kill the king by nigramancie and enchantemente," making an ointment to be put upon his saddle of such a nature that before he had ridden ten leagues he should swell up and die as he sat in his saddle. This was to be done with the aid of certain great prelates, and as soon as the king was dead Sir Thomas West would seize the Isle of Wight, the rector of Ashridge would raise the Chiltern men, and those of Wales and Chester should be summoned to rise by letters under the seal of Sir Edmund Mortimer, who was to be forced to head the rebellion. The same combination of magic and poison was said to have been intended against Henry VII on behalf of Perkin Warbeck, but with a rather larger pro-

portion of magic. According to Bernard de
Vignolles, John Kendal, Prior of the Knights
Hospitallers, Sir John Thweng, his nephew, and
Horsey, archdeacon of London, plotted against King
Henry and, being in Rome, consulted a Spanish
astrologer, Rodrigo, who couldn't help them, and
another, Master John, who showed his powers by
killing a Turk and then compounded a vile and
stinking ointment which he sent by Bernard to the
Prior, assuring him that if smeared on a doorway
or passage through which the king should pass it
would turn the hearts of his friends to betray and
murder him. Bernard, according to his own tale,
which was probably a lie, threw the stinking mess
into a jakes and substituted a mixture of quick-
silver and mud, over whose terrific properties he
waxed so eloquent that the Prior refused to have it
in his house and begged him to throw it away in
some distant spot.

This Spanish astrologer, who, by the way, was
remarkable for having lost his front teeth, but
offered to disguise himself with the aid of false
teeth of ivory, and take the poison to England
himself, if the conspirators would find the needful
funds—which they wouldn't—was an unusually
vicious specimen. As a whole, astrologers were
harmless, if not as necessary, as cats, and contented themselves with humble detective work;
but even such practices might have disastrous
effects when wrongful charges were brought
against innocent parties. When Cranbrook church
was robbed and the sexton killed in 1437, some of
the parishioners went to the " hosterye ycalled the
Horshedde " at Southwark and caused Master
Piers, a clerk, and John Bayly, a squire of the

Some Strange Tales

Duke of Gloucester, by witchcraft to accuse five innocent persons, as a result of which four had been " slayn myschief and distroied and ye fiveth as yn this world ys utterly undoo." Exactly what process of divination was used in this instance is not stated ; it may have been astrology or one of many other methods. A reference to a more uncommon and picturesque form of conjuration occurs in 1372, when John Crok of Tedworth was taken up for having in his possession a trunk with a man's head and a book in it. He explained that the head was that of a Saracen, and that he had bought it in Toledo in order to enclose a certain spirit in it so that the spirit should answer his questions. As he had not used it to defraud or deceive people he was released, on swearing not to use this or any other practice contrary to the holy faith ; but the marshal was ordered to burn the head, the book, and certain other scrolls of paper painted in different ways. A more usual method of divination, which differs from the last in having remained in common use to the present day,— for I have not heard that any of the Bond Street seers use a Saracen's head,—was crystal gazing. The medium, as a rule, was not a crystal but a mirror, but the principle remains the same, and, as is still the case with most Oriental seers, the actual scryer was often a child. Canon John Wilkinson, of Drax, whose adventures in search of the Mixendale hoard we have related, began his interest in magic in this way, for " whenne he was a child of xii yeres of age he was at an invocacion made at Wakefield by a scolar of Orlyaunce for a pair of bedes (that is to say, for a rosary which had been stolen), where he saw in a glasse a woman that had the beides in her hand, and a sprite crouned like a kyng in a chare of gold, and the clerke said he was a sprite," and he ought to have known, for what they didn't know at the University of Orleans about magic wasn't worth learning. The case of Peter Pemberton, a London vintner, who had John Mold arrested for theft on the evidence of " a man that loked in a glasse by the crafte of Nigromoncie,—whiche crafte by the lawe is dampned," is less satisfactory as he appears to have told the scryer whom he was to see. Still clearer is the evidence of fraud in the case of Thomas Notyngham, parish priest of Sprowston, "whiche was noysed a sothesayer." He was called in by Gregory Quentrell, of Norwich, expressly to identify Agnes Wattes as a thief, but, missing his cue, first accused one Margaret Wacy, who happened to be in the house, but upon Gregory's whispering in his ear, he changed his mind and, producing a book and a key, manipulated them so as to prove Agnes guilty. Luckily for her the constable of the ward happened to be passing, and he promptly haled the priest off before the warden of the city, where he admitted that he had " falsely lyed."

Divination by the book and key or by the sieve and shears was common enough amongst the wise women of the villages, and may not improbably still linger on in the more remote parts of the country, though its practice would no longer gain the user the reputation of being " a horse goodmother, water wych," or the more pleasant, but once defamatory, accusation " that she was a charmer." Such a charmer, or at least a conveyer of charm to others, was Mariot, of Belton, in the middle of the fifteenth century, who by her witchcraft claimed that she could cause lovesick damsels to obtain the husbands for whom they sighed. A charmer of another kind was Agnes Robson, just a century later. She cured, *deo mediante*, " little pigs and other animals " with this fine piece of gibberish :—" God almyghty, god and saincte charity. I beseche yow of your blessyd goodness to helpe this same thing, saying thus : John is thy xpen name. John and thre, bytter bytter hathe the bytten. Thre bytter bytter hathe the nyppen and thre bytter bytter hathe the stryken, besechyng almyghty god whedder it were eye or tong or hert the better shall be your heale and boote ; the father the son and the holy gooste." As an instance of a charm for human use, we may take the case of Janet Pereson, who told the mother of a sick child that it was " taken with the farye," and bade her send two persons to fetch southrunning water, which they were to bring back without speaking ; the child was to be washed in the water and its shirt dipped therein, and then hung upon a hedge at nightfall and in the morning the shirt would be gone, and the child cured. But something went wrong ; possibly the messengers spoke, or possibly the water was not running due south, or, still more probably, Janet couldn't find out which hedge the shirt was on ; anyhow, in the morning the shirt was still there, but whether the child was any the better for its wash is not said.

When we consider all the evidence for witchcraft, sorcery, and magic, as revealed in such records as these which I have strung together, we are left, I think, in a state of bewilderment as to how much was downright lying, how much lack of critical observation, and how much genuine fact.

Nor do I know any sovereign method of analysis. Human testimony is a tricky thing at best, and when given before a judge with the power of the Law or the Church behind him, is apt to reflect the presumed colour of the judge's mind rather than that of the witness. As the Abbot of Sawtry's servant declared after he had recited a story of miraculous visions—" iff that he be moved or induced to say that he believed other wayes, he wold peradventor say bifor Mr. Chaunceler that he beleved other wayes, but when Mr. Chaunceler were goon he saith he wold say to hymselff, ' goo foole goo,' and he saith that he wold bileve agayn as he dydd bifor."

XII. Birds

IN the somewhat dreary waste of official letters preserved in the Public Record Office, neatly mounted in red-bound volumes of impressive solidity, under the title of "Ancient Correspondence," one is occasionally rewarded by the discovery of a document containing some human and personal touch. One such that fell to my net recently was a letter from that worthy but asthmatic old lady, Eleanor of Provence, widow of Henry III, to her affectionate and dutiful son, Edward I. The letter, which is in that particular brand of French then in use at the English Court, thanks him for a present of cranes, which he had sent without their heads, and which she had found very fat and good.

It then continues :

" In regard that you desire us to let you know which we prefer, the bodies of the cranes without the heads or the heads without the birds ; we tell you that for us and for Monsire Huge le fuiz Otes the bodies are more suitable, but for you and Monsire Nicole de Coggeho the heads, because . . ."

At this critical place the fading of the ink has rendered additionally obscure a mild little joke of which the point was not particularly obvious in any case. If my deciphering is correct the reason given is " because your payments for cranes' heads cause them to be too highly seasoned (*trop bien saluz*)" and the reference is probably to the lavish rewards which Edward gave to the messengers who brought him the heads of the first cranes taken by hawks which were being trained for him. As an instance of his liberality we find that in 1290, when the servant of Sir John de Beauvent brought to the King at Querington, in Gloucestershire, the head of a crane which his gerfalcon " Calemare " had taken in Lindsay, he was given 6s. 8d. (equivalent to £4 10s. in modern money) " for the good news which he brought," and the same reward was given, in 1305, to Thomas Foukes, servant of Sir Robert de Bavant, bringing a crane's head to the King on behalf of his master, who was at this time one of the King's trainers.

There exists a number of Edward's letters written to Sir Robert in this same year, 1305, which show that the royal sportsman was well acquainted with the details of the elaborate process of training hawks, and took as much joy in issuing minute instructions in these matters as his father had done in matters of art or architecture. They also show that the culminating test of the falcon was its ability to take cranes, to which height it only rose after fleshing its talons on small waterfowl and winning its spurs in the pursuit of herons.

I am not sufficient naturalist to know whether the crane is still a frequent visitor to our shores, but I suspect that it is nearly as scarce as its unattractive relation, *Percnopterus*, of which, judging from the fact that it " never is content but whining and grumbling," the present habitat would seem to be on the north cliffs of Fleet Street.

Cranes must evidently have been fairly plentiful in the eastern counties in the fourteenth century, though as they were sometimes bought for sporting purposes, it is possible that they were also imported. As they were in the habit of leaving windy Ilium and the Hellespont at the approach of winter, and sudden rains, for the warmth of Africa, and the excitement of waging war with the Pigmies, I should have supposed that they would only have been found in England during the summer, and I admit I am puzzled to find Edward writing on March 11 to the effect that the craning season is passing. Possibly, however, the Hellespontine cranes of Homer, flying in noisy, chattering crowds, differed in habits from the wilier cranes of later date and most westerly origin, who obtained the double advantage of ballast against winds and silence, best of shields for a plump and defenceless bird, by carrying stones in their bills during their migrations.

In one of these letters to Bavant, King Edward expresses himself as much annoyed to hear that some of his gerfalcons are turning out badly and that one in particular seems hopeless. Such disappointments were often the lot of the hawker, and just three hundred years later we find the Earl of Shrewsbury writing apologetically to Sir Robert Cecil about a laner hawk, which he had obtained for him on somebody else's recommendation—" she is but a slugg, now being commended to you for so rare and excellent a bird," adding, after various disparaging remarks " the next hawk I commend unto you before my own eyes have seen her fly, shall be made of orient pearl." It must have been a bird of the same type that the great Cecil had himself given a few years before to Sir Edward Winter, who acknowledged the gift with more candour than courtesy : " Your Barbary falcon I received, which if I should praise very much you would rather commend me for a courteous knight than a skilful falconer. But, howsoever, I thank you for her, though I think she be dead or this."

Another fact which the Edwardian records bring out is that Dame Julian Bernes, earliest of literary sportswomen, was merely indulging her fancy in drawing up a list of the several kind of hawks apportioned to the several ranks of society. Edward did indeed use the gerfalcons which she assigns to kings, but he did not despise the laner of the esquires or the goshawk of the yeomen, while the falcon gentle, which Dame Julian would reserve for dukes, was certainly used at this time by knights. When, in 1280, the villeins of Harewick, exasperated by the oppressions of their lord, Sir Simon de Pierpoint, rose up and sacked his house, they tore his tabard, beat his charger, and slew his gentle falcon, and it would be easy to show that no such hard-and-fast classification existed in fact, either at that date or at the end of the fifteenth century, when the lady wrote. Oddly enough, Dame Julian's opening class of eagles for emperors, which sounds improbable, had some justification, for " the Muscovian emperors reclaime eagles to fly at hindes, foxes, etc., and such a one was sent as a present for Queen Elizabeth."

Eagles would occasionally attack the lesser birds of prey, but on some occasions, if the medieval naturalists are to be trusted, the intelligence of the quarry proved too much for the brute force of the kingly pursuer. At Rouen, in the twelfth century, an eagle having killed one of a pair of falcons,

Birds

the survivor, anticipating the tactics of Judson with his flat-iron gun-boat, enticed his enemy to pursue him closely and diving suddenly through a small hole in a wooden bridge, had the satisfaction of hearing the eagle crash in fatal haste against the timber. Yet we must not fall into the error of regarding the eagle as a stupid bird, for " subtile shee is and wittie, for when shee hath seezed upon tortoises and caught them up with her tallons shee throweth them downe from aloft to breake their shels." It must be admitted that this particular example of her wit partakes rather of the nature of practical joking, and especially so in the famous case of the poet Æschylus, upon whose bald head an eagle dropped a tortoise with disastrous accuracy.

Returning once more to Edward I we find him not only getting the assistance of Sir Robert de Bavant and expressing his thanks to Dame Mary de Merke for the care she had taken of " our falcon Marmaduke," but also addressing his thanks and his supplications to higher quarters. Quite early in his reign he laid down the rule that when a new falcon took its first crane, 13d. should be given in alms *pro Deo*, and there are a number of cases in which pilgrimages were undertaken for the health of sick hawks. Occasionally the birds themselves were carried to the shrines, but more often their images in wax—no rough and ready puppets, but models carefully fashioned and painted by the King's own goldsmith, were sent ; or, in less serious cases, a silver penny would be bent over the head of the bird in honour of some saint, at whose altar the penny was then offered. Chief of the pilgrimage shrines for the royal hawks were those of

More Medieval Byways

St. Thomas Cantelupe, at Hereford, and of the more famous St. Thomas Becket, at Canterbury. Why Cantelupe should have been chosen is not clear, but Becket had been a thorough sportsman in his early days and as a lad had almost lost his life in Pevensey Level, trying to rescue a drowning hawk. He had also, on several occasions, long before King Edward's time, miraculously saved the sick or injured hawks of his devotees, and even exerted his powers on behalf of Guiscard, the favourite falcon of his old adversary, Henry II. For the matter of that, Becket was not above aiding even humbler fowl, and when some boys at Canterbury, having plucked a dead gander, threw it into a corner, scoffingly commending it to St. Thomas, the Saint promptly restored it to life. As, however, he did not complete the miracle by restoring its feathers, the result was unsatisfactory to the gander, though it redounded greatly to the honour of the Saint, being authenticated by the testimony of the monks, who received it and—less considerate than the old lady who made flannel jackets for the geese which she had plucked while they were stupefied with cherry brandy—ate it. After all, the goose has, for all its alleged stupidity, no mean reputation. Apart from saving the Capitol geese have displayed an affectionate attachment to humans, comparable to that shown by the swan of St. Hugh of Lincoln, though it is true that Pliny, while recording these touching incidents, puts a higher value on their livers than on their hearts, and commends the Consul Scipio Metellus as the first inventor of *pâté de foie gras*, " that great good and singular commodite to mankind."

In another miracle of St. Thomas, a starling

escaped from the talons of a hawk by uttering a pious invocation of the saint, which its master had taught it. This ability of birds to imitate the human voice appealed to the ancients and, if we can hardly accept Pliny's statement that Drusus and Germanicus had nightingales which could speak Latin and Greek, there are plenty of more authentic stories of talking birds. It was a talking raven that, after it had been murdered by its master's rival, was accorded a magnificent public funeral by the populace of Rome, an honour which has probably never befallen any other bird, with the possible exception of the Egyptian Ibis, most sacred and cautious of birds. (*Medio tutissimus ibis*, " In the midst is the ibis, most cautious of birds.") But far ahead of chough, magpie, jackdaw, starling, or raven, in oratory, was the gorgeous popinjay, now shorn of half his romance by his commonplace appellation of parrot. There is a pleasant story of a crusading knight, who, wandering on the shore near the popinjay-haunted slopes of Mount Gilboa, called out in jest to one bird : " Our popinjay in its cage at home, who is very like you, sends you greeting," whereupon the bird addressed fell down in a swoon. Returning home to England the knight told his story to his admiring family, when suddenly his own popinjay, who had been listening intently, gave a dismal squawk and fell from its perch. Efforts to revive it were vain and it died, though whether from shock or from the effort to swallow its master's tale is not quite clear. Other equally veracious incidents connected with the bird's knowledge of the human tongue might be retailed, but it is more surprising to find that " popingayes, nightingales and other sweete

singyng birds" are not infrequently classed
together. Indeed, in a tale of two squires of
Falmouth, of whom " the one was dampnyd for
breakyng his wedlock the tother was savyd," we
may read how " tother " was escorted to the gates
of Heaven, where :

> " They harde upon the yates on high
> Mynstralsy and Angelle song ;
> The Pellycan and the popynjaye
> The tymor and the turtill trewe
> An hondrede thousande in ther laye,
> The nyghtyngale with notes newe."

Neither the pelican nor the turtle-dove is usually
classed in the first rank of singing birds, though they
are both of unblemished character, and, indeed,
proverbial for piety and chastity. I can therefore
only assume that they, and the popinjay, which
resembles the Pauline bishop in being the " husband of one wife," were admitted to the heavenly
choir, as members are to country choirs, for moral
rather than vocal excellence. On the other hand,
if there were anything approaching a hundred
thousand popinjays singing together, my memories
of the parrot-house at the Zoo induce me to believe
that the poet was mistaken, and that they had
reached the gates, not of Heaven, but of—to
employ the euphemism used in the House of
Commons when speaking of the House of Lords—
" another place."

XIII. Beasts ～ ～ ～ ～ ～

"AMONG those domesticall creatures that converse with us there be many thinges worth the knowledge," some of which we may consider, beginning with the most domesticated of animals, the dog. In few things is the contrast between the peoples of the East and of the West more marked than in their attitude towards dogs. In Eastern literature, sacred and profane, the lowest image of contempt is the dog, though why " the Turkes colour their dogs' tails with red" I do not know ; nor can I say whether in this ancient custom is to be found the origin of the red tail light which, in recent times, has spread even to our bicycles. Homer seemes to have shared the Asiatic dislike of the dog, and " dog-face " is one of the expressive terms in the rich vocabulary of abuse which his heroes or Billingsgate goddesses hurl at one another. On the other hand, the young lady who wrote the Odyssey and fathered it on Homer made some amends by introducing the touching picture of the faithful old hound who recognised his master, Odysseus, on his return from his long wanderings in disguise. Among the later Greeks, as civilisation advanced, the keeping of pet dogs seems to have come in, and as Dr. Cay, better known in Cambridge and the medical world as Caius, made " a certain abridgement of Dogs," so Alcibiades cut off his dog's tail and thus " curtailed the already cur-tailed cur " to give the Athenians something to talk about. Coming down to later times, and a more Western race, we find dogs of all kinds and sizes popular as pets with the Romans, and Pliny has much to say about them. Possibly he is correct in his statement that " the bitch-whelpe that commeth of the first litter sees strange bugs and goblins," at any rate I once had a dog that was always looking for strange fleas, and the Rabbinical authorities were all agreed that dogs could see the Angel of Death, while some of my friends have had strange experiences with phantom collies and retrievers ; and if a dog can be a ghost, why should he not see one ? Not only can a dog become a ghost, but it is on record that one became a saint. The Breton greyhound, Guinefort, of whom a story is told of misjudged heroism and martyrdom exactly similar to the well-known legend of the Welsh hound, Gelert, attained such fame that its burial place became known as the tomb of St. Guinefort, where miracles were wrought and superstitious rites, more pagan than pious, were practised. There was another hound which obtained posthumous fame of a kind, but by no means the odour of sanctity, the brach " Jolyf," whose body the Friars of Berwick flung into a well to annoy the townsmen—in which they were successful. But this by the way.

Of big dogs, of the type that is " lightly angry and byteth gladly strange dogges," the hunting and poaching dogs, medieval records have much to say, but of the " smalle ladye's popees that bere awaie the fleas " not so much. One would like to know something of the " couple of little fayre houndes " presented to Princess Mary of bloody memory, and still more of the " cute little dog " (*parvum canem cautum*) given to Prince Edward of

Beasts

Carnarvon, in 1290, by the Lady Joan, ankaress of Blyth. No doubt they were something in the nature of the " Spaniel gentle " that " Puppetly and pleasant cur (which some frumpingly tearm Fysting Hound)," which one older writer denounced as " a silly shift to shun irksome idleness " on the part of their " minsing mistresses," serving no useful purpose except to act as live plaisters, or hot-water bottles, and so ease internal discomforts.

Dogs naturally suggest the subject of cats, and both a dog and a cat formed an essential part of a medieval ship's equipment, even before the Mayoralty of Richard Whittington, and were so far recognised as members of the crew that if either escaped alive from a wrecked ship the ship was not regarded as derelict, and the owner could recover any goods saved from it. Earlier still the superiority of the cat over the dog is marked in the ancient laws of Wales, according to which a cat ranked with a cock and a bull as the live stock essential for the constitution of a proper hamlet. It says much for the strongly marked and unchanging individuality of the cat that those extraordinarily inaccurate persons who wrote on alleged natural history in medieval days have, for the most part, hit off her characteristics with unusual fidelity. Two writers have between them anticipated in brief the story of the " Cat that Walked by Itself," the one stating that " Once cats were all wild, but afterwards they retired to houses," the other adding that " He doth delighte that he enjoyeth his libertie " : in which two sentences the whole of Mr. Kipling's story is condensed. Naturally those two outstanding features of the cat, its eyes and its voice, come in for their share of attention. " Her eyes glisten above measure, especially when a man cometh to see them on a suddain, and in the night they can hardly be endured for their flaming aspect," and moreover she has " a peculiar direful voice," or as another more descriptive writer puts it, " he maketh a rueful noyse and ghastful when one proffereth to fight with another." As a pet, the cat seems medievally to have been appreciated only by witches and wizards, while as a mouser its place was largely taken by the unattractive weasel, which was more energetic in its pursuit of mice and more terrible to them, insomuch that when mice heard its cry " they all fall astonished." In spite of moral anecdotes which show the weasel to be a model mother and remarkably intelligent, I cannot picture it as a satisfactory substitute for either the frolicsome kitten or the comfortable fireside cat. Even the knowledge that " a vulgar weasel being kept very old and drunk in wine " is an excellent remedy for snake bites, and that the weasel itself, although it has not studied at Salerno or Montpellier, is expert in herb lore, leaves me unreconciled to its lean and hungry look.

A little of the weasel's herb lore would have been useful to the asses of Thuscia and would have prevented their eating hemlock, after indulging in which they " sleep so long and strangely that oftentimes the country men begin to flea them, and on the suddain, their skins half taken off the other half on, they awake braying in such a horrible manner that the poor men are most dreadfully affrighted therewith."

The sympathy in this case seems to be misplaced, for though " their voice is very rude and frightful "

Beasts

it is hardly to be expected that they should be polite in such singularly unpleasant circumstances. That asses could, upon occasion, behave with dignity and discretion we must suppose from the fact that Ammonian always had an ass in to hear his lectures on philosophy, in which respect that ancient professor seems to have incurred deliberately the undesired experience of many modern lecturers at Oxford, if not at Cambridge.

While philosophy is the domain of men and asses, mathematics of the Elberfeld horses, and Greek, if Pliny is to be believed, of elephants and nightingales, music has a far wider appeal and " comfortyth bestis, and serpentes, foules and delphines," but particularly deer. This innocent delight in music, and their unsuspicious curiosity—for bucks, both cervine and human, " are very simple and foolish creatures, amused, yea and amased, they will be at everything and keep a-wondering at it," —have often been used for their capture. One form of deer, however, the Tarandus, which seems to have been the reindeer " with variations," as a musician would say, is alleged to have found safety in protective colouring, changing its hues to resemble its surroundings, like a chameleon, or perhaps still more like a modern politician, for " when he list to look like himselfe and be in his owne colour he resembleth an Asse."

In the matter of colour schemes the writer of the rhyme :

" I never saw a purple cow, I never want to see one,
But I can tell you anyhow, I'd rather see than be one,"

probably thought that he had reached the limit of absurdity.   He does not seem to have realised that in Æthiopia there are, or perhaps it would be safer to say were, " kine of a purple colour which have but one horn growing out of their heads." There was also, of course, the famous Dun Cow of War-wick, but she was remarkable more for her size and ferocity than for her colour, and may have been a descendant of those cows of the Phœnicians which " were so high that a very tall man could not milk them except he stood upon a footstool." Of the common or farmyard cow much might be said if space allowed. Most people know by experience that " olde beefe and kowe-flesshe doth ingender melancolye," but, while the nutritive value of calf's foot jelly is fairly notorious, probably few realise that " the ancle of a white cow laid forty daies and nights into wine and rubbed on the face with white lint taketh spotts and maketh the face look very clean." Equally rare is the knowledge that a man who has lost his eyebrows or eyelashes can grow a fresh crop by holding his face over a lighted candle made of paper and cow's marrow. Oddly enough, the milk, which we should consider the chief excellence of the cow, was not highly praised, except for making butter, being considered too fatty and especially bad for " them which have gurgulacyons in the bely." Even for making cheese it was held inferior to sheep's milk, though superior to that of " the vulgar bugil," a beast almost, if not quite, identical with that " vengeable beast " the bovy of Bohemia, whose milk " maketh very hard cheese which tasteth like earth." Goat's milk was much more commended and was used by Edward I in his old age, a small herd of goats accom-panying him on his journeys and military expeditions and next to it ranked the milk of the sheep.

Beasts

The sheep, on whose fleece England's national credit and her Lords Chancellors have alike reposed, had some claim to oust the more decorative heraldic leopard from the proud position of being England's beast, at least in her own opinion, for she held that :

> " Nouther Tigre, Oliphant nor Griffin—
> All thynges rekned through every region—
> Doth so gret profite, hors nor goose nor swan,
> As doth the sheepe unto the ese of man."

Of the rivals thus condemned, the horse and the goose had their opinion of their own merits, and stated them at great length, and the swan was introduced obviously rather with an eye to rhyme than as a serious competitor. Of the first three creatures named, the elephant might have made out a good case for himself in his native land, but the griffin and the tiger were ravening beasts who would have found it difficult to call any witnesses to give them a good character ; they were, in fact, in the same class with the beautiful and sweet-savoured panther, of whom one ungallant writer says : " We have already said that they most resemble women, and indeed they are enemies to all creatures." So ferocious was the panther that he was a terror even to the dragon, but, on the other hand, he was himself afraid of that mean beast, the hyena. In the same way the lion was notoriously terrified of a white cock and " discouraged by snakes " ; and harts, while " valiant against serpents, are naturally afraid of hares and conies and will not fight with them." Which is a pity, as the spectacle of a stand-up fight between the Monarch of the Glen and that "wilde and skippish beast," the hare, would be an astonishment and a joy to the beholders. It should also follow as a matter of pure mathematics, that if the lion is afraid of snakes, which are afraid of harts, which are afraid of hares, then much more will the lion be afraid of a hare. "Which," as Euclid remarks, "is absurd."

XIV. Fish ❧ ❧ ❧ ❧ ❧

"OF all nacyons and countres, England is beste servyd of Fysshe, not only of al manner of see-fysshe, but also of fresshe-water fysshe, and of al manner of sortes of salte-fysshe." There was therefore a certain propriety and national significance in the banquet given by Henry V in honour of his marriage with gentle Kate of France, for "ye shall understande that this feest was all of fysshe." Some idea of the Lenten resources of medieval England can be gathered from the menu of the three courses, each consisting of a dozen or more dishes, which constituted that memorable banquet. All kinds of fish were represented, from fried minnows to "fresshe sturgeon with welkes," and in particular a host of the lesser and now despised fresh-water fish, including roach, perch, gudgeon, chub (about as appetising as an old pair of boots and probably less sustaining), and tench ("of a most unclean and damnable nourishment "). Salmon and "trought" each make a single appearance, but the only fish that occurs in all three courses is the regicide lamprey. Undeterred by the fate of Henry I, monarchs and nobles continued to patronise the luscious lamprey. Henry III, in one of his curiously intimate official notes, orders supplies of this delicacy to be sent up to Westminster, "because to the king and queen all other fish seem insipid beside lampreys." However they were devoted to lampreys after their death, our kings do not seem to have considered them lovely and pleasant in their lives, and even Henry III, with his genius for selecting undesirable favourites, did not follow the example of the Roman orator, Hortensius, who made a pet of a lamprey and wept over its death, or of Antonia, wife of Drusus, who bedecked one of her lampreys with jewels, including earrings, doubtfully appropriate to a fish traditionally connected by marriage, if not by blood, with the " deaf adder who stoppeth her ears." Unattractive, as most would consider, when alive, the lamprey, when cooked must have excelled even the conger, of which one ancient enthusiast declared that the savour was so divine that it would make a dead man sniff.

In the matter of cooking fish the Scots, in the sixteenth century, held the highest reputation, and it is possible that they were among the rare cooks who could even make a savoury pie out of the dry, unappetising, stockfish, which the Icelanders, " beastly creatures, unmanered and untaughte," used to eat raw. Nor was this skill of the Scots to be despised in days when fasting was universal and fishing was the pursuit of food and not a form of sport. For the average gentleman of the Middle Ages would have agreed with Plutarch in regarding fishing as " a filthy, base, illiberable imployment having neither wit nor perspicacity in it." Occasionally a great man would attend the dragging or netting of his stews ; for instance, the Abbot of Fountains had a lake where he sometimes fished in person, on which occasions a horn would be blown to summon the neighbouring tenants to assist, in return for which they received half the catch ; but the growth of angling as a form of sport was slow. An exceptionally early reference in the Willoughby

household accounts of 1521 to 8d. paid " for
ownttment to take fyche " seems to anticipate the
" alluring ointments " of the later seventeenth
century, concocted of cat's fat, powdered mummy,
oil from a dead man's skull, and similar abomina-
tions, but it was not until the time of the Stuarts
that men began to feel, with the Silesian nobleman,
that it was as good to hunt carp as hares and
abandoned the net for the rod and line. Incid -
tally the common belief that carps, hops, and the
Reformation came into England together appears
questionable, as carp appears in English cookery
books of earlier date and " carpe deore," which
suggests goldfish, was served at the banquet of
Henry V.

If the carp is the wiliest of pond fish, surely the
mullet, for which Arundel early attained a great
celebrity, must be the most foolish of sea-fish, for
" the mullets have a naturall ridiculous qualitie
by themselves to be laughed at ; for when they be
afraid to be caught they hide their heads, and then
they thinke they bee sure ynough, weening that
their bodies is likewise hidden." A certain fortunate foolishness was also noticeable in the shark,
whose attention was easily attracted away from
his prey, so that if a sailor fell overboard and was
attacked by a shark, his mates would throw over a
dummy figure of straw in a white garment, presumably kept handy for this express purpose, and
the shark would at once turn to this and leave the
man free to escape. That all fish were not foolish,
however, is easily seen from the cunning displayed
by the " sea-frog " in obtaining a meal. " It
puddereth in the mud and troubleth the water
that it might not be seene ; and when the little

seely fishes come skipping about her, then she puts out her little hornes or barbels which she hath bearing forth under her eies, and by little and little tilleth and tolleth them so neere that she can easily seaze upon them." Wisdom and beauty do not always go together and this sea-frog is an ugly devil, uglier even than the flounder, whose side-drawn mouth perpetuates the sneer with which he received the election of the herring as king of fishes.

Making allowance for the silvery beauty of a shoal of herring and for the excellence of " baken herynge dressid and digt with white sugure," or of the pies that Norwich sent yearly to the King, made of herrings, dressed with ginger, cloves, cinnamon, galingale and other spices, most people would still be inclined to confer the title of royalty upon the salmon. What occult connexion there can be between that lordly fish and the pig, I cannot say, but I believe it is still considered unlucky for a salmon fisher to mention pigs, and in a Scottish Statute of the twelfth century a free passage, without nets or traps, had to be left in midstream of a salmon river so wide that a three-year old sow, well-fed, could not touch both sides at once, while a century later the passage in the Derwent was to be wide enough for a sow and her five little ones to pass through. In case of disputes the difficulty of applying such a legal standard to the measurement of the stream must have been extraordinary, as anyone who has attempted to get five little pigs into line on land will admit. The idea of these river pigs naturally suggests the sea-swine, porpoises or porkpisce, which " hath his name from the hog hee resembles in convexity and

curvyte of his backe, from the head to the tayle."
Oddly enough the porpoise, " nother praysed in
the olde testament nor in physycke," was regarded
by our ancestors as excellent eating, its tongue
being apparently considered as an especial dainty,
as Henry I, when he granted the Bishop of London
the right to all " craspeis " taken on his estate,
carefully added, " except the tongue, which I have
reserved to myself." This, being, like the sturgeon and the whale, a royal fish, was usually
claimed by the Crown, and in the sixteenth century
a complaint was made from Devon that while
there was " yerely grete resorte of the fysche called
Porpes, whereof yf any by chance happyn to be
takyn the officers of the Admiraltie compell the
pore men fyschers of the same to pay and delyvere
them of every of the said fysche the tone half,"
so that now no one would trouble to catch them.
For the purposes of medieval unnatural history
the porpoise was identified with the dolphin, that
most musical or rather music-loving, of fish, which
" hath no voyce but singeth like a man," and also
resembles many men of the type who cannot but do
sing, in that " it slepeth very hartely, that thei be
heard ronke (snore) a farre off." The musical
ability of the porpoise was conspicuously displayed at the choral festival held " when Myd-
somer evyn fell on Palmes Soundey," for then :

" The samon sang the hie Mass, the heryng was his
    clerk,
  On the organs playde the porpas, ther was a mery
    werke."

If its appearance as a performer was exceptional,
it was an excellent listener, for though it has

" none ears for to here, nor no nose for to smelle, yet it smelleth very welle and sharpe, and they here gladly playnge on instruments, as lutes, harpes, tabours and pypes." A similar taste on the part of the whale was used for its capture. " When the maryners spie where he is, then their accompanye them a gret many of shyppes togeder about him with divers instrementis of musike, and they playe with grete armonye " (being apparently more handy with the harp than Kipling's jolly mariners) " and the fische is very glad of this armonye and cometh fletynge above the waters to here the melody ; then they have among them an instrument of yron, the whiche they fasten into the harde skinne and the weght of it synkrth downwards into the fat and grese, and sodenly with that all the instruments of musik be stylle." While this may have been the procedure of the regular whalers, the medieval sailor was not above dispensing with the orchestra and improvising a harpoon, and in 1280 the tenants of the Countess of Arundel are recorded to have pursued a whale off the coast of Norfolk, " with their anchors fixed in it." It was off the same coast in 1255 that a " great monstrous fish," probably a sperm whale, was captured after a struggle in which six boats were sunk. Whale steak is a delicacy of which one still reads in records of Arctic exploration, but it was formerly a common and much appreciated dish in England ; there are frequent orders for a whale to be sent up from the coast to the royal larder or for " 100 pieces of best whale," for the King's table, while at the end of the thirteenth century, whale " of this year's salting " fetched 2d. a pound, and " super-

Fish

annuated " whale (a most unattractive item for a
fish dinner) cost half that price.   Seal was another
of the " deynteithes full dere " of past generations, but most of us would probably be content to
ignore the meaty part of the seal, while appreciating
his skin and deprecating his marital habits, for he
" fighteth ever with his wyfe tyll she be dede and
when he hath kylled her seketh another and liveth
with her very well tyl he dye."   Which seemes to
be an argument in favour of second marriages.

When the seal set so bad an example of behaviour
it is not surprising that the little fishes of the sea
should occasionally have been lacking in refine-
ment.   The plaice, for instance, " is a fisshe that
is in sandy grounde, and when he is moved or
stered he wynketh," just as Alice's " eldest oyster
winked his eye and shook his heavy head."   Still
more vulgar was the behaviour of the murex, that
species of whelk from which the Tyrian purple dye
was obtained and which was therefore called the
purple : " When a cockle gapes the purples make
at them with their pointed tongue, which they
thrust out to annoy them."   No wonder that
Browning asked : " Who brought the murex up ? "
Of course, to some extent, the cockles may be said
to have provoked the purples by gaping, and they
were fortunate to escape with insult and avoid the
injury which befell the equally unmannerly oyster,
of which it is said that " when the oyster gapeth
the crab throweth lytell stones in him and so
getteth his fishe out, for it bydeth then open."
Talking of crabs reminds one that, contrary to
what might be expected, the lobster is subject to
nerves and can be frightened to death, for while,
" lobsters are readie to scratch and teare the congre;

the congres againe doe as much for the polype; yet, the lobster if so afraid of the polype or pourcuttell that if he spie him neere he evermore dieth for very woe." In this case the antipathy was no doubt justifiable as a large octopus or cuttlefish might be more than a match for a lobster, but why on earth should a wolf be afraid of a shrimp? Yet it was.

XV. *De Minimis* ❧ ❧ ❧ ❧

"PETRUS GALLISARDUS, Caelius Chalcagninus, and Tzetzes are reported to have
written the 'Commendation of a Flea'; it was my
desire to have seen this, but it was never my
chance." So wrote Dr. Muffet—the Elizabethan
authority on insects and, presumably, father of
the young lady whose rural banquet was rudely
disturbed by one of those spiders, which her father
declared were themselves excellent articles of diet,
adducing in proof thereof the fact that "we have
in England a great lady yet living who will not
leave off eating them." I also have failed to find
this commendation; nor am I even clear whether
each of the three vied with the others in praise of
that skippish and irreverent insect, or whether there
were not three commendations but one commendation—a joint eulogy, even perchance a complete
opus, libretto by Chalcagninus, lyrics by Tzetzes,
and music by Gallisardus. What did they find
to praise in fleas? Perhaps their habit of early
rising—a detestable virtue, which tends to produce
an odious self-complacency in those who practise
it—for "so soon as day breaks they forsake the
bed." Let it, at least, be accounted to them for
virtue that they do not get out of bed at that unholy
hour from any foolish belief in the merit of such a
habit, but because they know their deeds are evil
and they are urged by that instinct of self-preser-
vation, thanks to which "when they finde they are
arraigned to die and they feel the finger coming, on

a sudden they are gone and leap here and there and so escape the danger." Excellent Bartholomew, who, with a fine broad interest in the affairs of the universe, wrote " Of the Nature of Things " in the twelfth century, tells us—in words that reveal how little evolution has affected either fleas or kings in seven centuries—that the flea " is a lyttell worme of wonder lyghtnes and scapethe and voydeth peryll with leypnge and not with rennynge, and wexeth slow and fayleth in colde tyme, and in somer tyme it wexeth quiver and swyft. . . . And the flee is bredde whyte and chaungeth as hit were sodeynlye in to blacke colour and desyreth blode and byteth and percethe therfore and styngeth the fleshe that he sytteth on, and doth lette them that wolde slepe with sharpe bytyng and spareth not kynges, but a lyttell flee greveth them if he touche theyr fleshe."

Nor would the little democrat reverence even the sacrosanct person of an ambassador, as the Bishop of Norwich had rueful reason to realise when he was sent by Henry II to Sicily. Wiser travellers than the episcopal ambassador carried with them, in pre-Keating days, powdered flea-bane, which " by its smell doth astonish the Fleas that they will not bite." Failing such protection, one could only pray that one's visitors might belong to the older generation ; for, " the lesser, the leaner and the younger they are, the sharper they bite ; the fat ones play and tickle men more willingly,"— which reminds one of the pleasing remark of the French lady, " Quant à moi, ce n'est pas la morsure, c'est la promenade."

In sharp contrast to the amiable, plethoric, and elderly flea, " Tykes will sometimes enter deep into the skin with their nose." (Though this was written of sheep-ticks it is also true of Yorkshire tykes.) This unpleasant insect's cousin, the louse, "is a beastly Creature and known better in Innes and Armies than it is Wellcome," and the only thing that can be said in its favour is that in medieval times, when godliness and cleanliness were at opposite poles, it kept good company, being the constant companion of saints. The hair shirt of St. Yves of Brittany, who died in the odour of what his admirers declared was sanctity, was a crawling horror even to his contemporaries, and when its inhabitants fell out he would gently replace them, saying "Let them go back into their warren." At a later date, "Functius the Governour of Zurich was like to have written a commendation of wall-lice in medicine," but apparently his heart failed him.

In comparison with such as these the fly is almost admirable. They love the obscene dark which the fly detests, while "the light, like Truth, he doth exceedingly rejoyce in, and doth behave himself honestly therein and civilly"—or apparently did in Elizabethan times, for his manners have shockingly deteriorated. Tzetzes, whose sympathy with flies might be prognosticated from his very name, declared with more imagination than accuracy that "such is their love to those of their own kind that they bury their dead corpses"; if they do so at all, I imagine it must be in much the same way that certain cannibal tribes put away their dear departed. It is a notable peculiarity of the fly that "he doth not sting with a sting as the Bee and the Wasp do, but with his mouth snout like the Elephant." Personally, I have been

More Medieval Byways

so fortunate as never yet to have been stung by
an elephant, but judging by my experience of
certain strangely variegated flies of approximately
similar magnitude in the Rhone Valley [1] I should
imagine that it would be unpleasant. Most people
have their own pet deterrent, with which they
besmalm themselves, or more frequently their
friends, but farmers may be grateful for the
information that cattle can be protected from the
attacks of flies by anointing them with lion's
grease. If the butcher should happen to be out
of lion fat, which comes under the heading of offal
and was therefore never subject to government
control, the juice of wild marjoram is said to be an
efficient substitute. Travellers in the East will
also do well to remember that just as earth from
the grave of the prophet Jeremiah keeps away
crocodiles so " Crocodile broth chaseth away
flies " ;—one of those merciful dispensations of
Providence by which bane and antidote are to be
found in close proximity, crocodiles and flies being
alike most troublesome in such countries as Egypt.
Yet even Egypt in the days of Moses can hardly
have witnessed such a sight as was seen at Tewkesbury on February 24, 1575, when, after a slight
flood, " in the afternoone there came downe the
river of Avon great numbers of flies and beetles,
such as in sommer evenings use to strike men in
the faces, in great heaps, a foote thicke above the
water so that to credible mens judgement there
were seene within a payre of Buts-lengths of
those flyes above an hundred quarters. The mills

[1] Upon discussing this point with the friend who was with
me on that occasion, he declares that I have exaggerated the
dimensions of these flies and that they were really little, if at
all, bigger than sheep.

De Minimis

thereabouts were damned up with them for the space of 4 dayes after, and then were clensed by digging them out with shovels : from whence they came is yet unknowne, but the day was colde, and a hard frost."

Classical scholars need not be reminded that, while Homer finds in the fly a simile (correct but unconvincing) for the reckless and persistent valour of the Greeks, Ælian "inveighs against their procacity and sauciness," and Plutarch, whose portraits, if I remember right, show him to have been bald, complains that they " do not shew the least courtesie or the least shew of a grateful minde for what they receive of any man." These sons of Baalzebub might learn a lesson from the devotion of one of the smallest and most musical of their tribe, the gnat who, seeing a snake about to bite that other sweet singer, Virgil, settled on the poet's ear and stung with all his strength. Virgil, who seems to have excelled the common race of men as much in quickness of hand as in the turning of hexameters, sat up and slapped and slew the gnat, while, as Milton remarked on another occasion, " Back to the thicket slunk the guilty serpent." That night the ghost of the gnat visited Virgil, and the next morning the remorseful poet returned to the scene of his slumbers, buried the corpse of his preserver with appropriate rites, and composed an elegy " De Culice."

Another kindly creature is the mantis, whose pious pose of uplifted hands sceptical naturalists now assure us is an attitude of preying and not of prayer. Earlier and more sympathetic observers knew better, and saw in her Nature's anticipation of the London policeman, for " if a child aske the way to such a place, she will stretch out one of her feet and show him the right way and seldome or never misse." Similar consideration for children is also to be found in a quarter where we should little expect it ; for the admirable Muffet assures us that " all little Worms found in prickly herbs, if any meat stick in the narrow passage of the throat of children, will presently help them." In this connection " One Samuel Quickelbergius, a learned young man, saith—as I was gathering of Simples, a certain old man came unto me whilst I sought for a little Worm in the head of the Fullers Teazill, and he said unto me, ' O thou happy young man, if thou didst but certainly know the secret vertues of that little Worm, which are many and great.' And when I entreated him that he would acquaint me with them, he held his peace and by no intreaty could I obtain it of him." The greater part of this precious secret, it is to be feared, died with the mysterious old man, though we do know that this particular worm is almost as good a remedy for toothache as spiders' eggs mixed with spike oil. Talking of worms, " I need not contend that there are worms in small Nuts for all men know it : it is strange that Ringelbergius writes, that these worms may be fed to be as big as a Serpent, with sheeps milk, yet Cardanus considers the same and shewes the way to feed them." This experiment, however, is hardly worth the trouble, except as a matter of curiosity, for few people are really fond of worms, however large, and most of us are more anxious to diminish than to increase them. While such diminution may be effected with some of the patent poisons employed with

horrid success on golf greens, it may be as well to
bear in mind that more romantic methods are
available for men of adventurous spirit, and
especially for those who have had experience in
raiding trenches, for " it is good also in tempes-
tuous and dark nights to go into gardens silently,
and to creep upon them, by the help of fire carried
in a horn : for so in one night thousands of them
may be intercepted and killed."

That " worme of slyme," the snail, which " is a
right slowe worme in mevynge and is a manner
snake and beareth an harde shelle on his backe
and closeth him therin and is an horned worm,"
was not distinguished by name from his houseless
brother, the slug, until comparatively recent times.
For once the animal creation has got back some of
its own, and, in revenge for the derogatory use of
the titles of donkey, pig, and goose applied to
mankind, that loathly worm is called after the
human " slugge who lokyth to be holpe of God
that commawndyth men to waake in the worlde."
Moreover, our friend Bartholomew has introduced
a further confusion by anticipating Mr. Punch's
railway porter and asserting that " the Tortuse is
accounted among snailes, for he is closed betwene
mooste harde shelles." But then Bartholomew's
strongest point was not scientific classification and
he lumps together all kinds of caterpillars and
glow-worms under the name of " the Malshragge,"
which he describes, in words which all gardeners
who have to squash these juicy marauders will
admit are horribly true, as " a neshe worme and full
of matter, distyngued with divers colours, shynynge
as a sterre by nyghte, and hath many colours and
foule shape by daye " ; while he goes on to assert

that it becomes " a fleeyng worme hyghte Papilio."
On the subject of butterflies he is inclined to think
that they should be called "smale foules," but
quotes Papias as saying that they "be smalle
fleenge beastes that come by nyghte when lighte
is kyndled in candelles and labour to quenche the
light of the candels, and so they be brent in the
fyre of the candelles, and somtyme when they
laboure to destroye lyghte of other bestes, they are
punyshed and hurte in their owne bodys"—an
explanation of their foolish behaviour which may
serve to moderate our sympathy at their fate.
No distinction was made before the eighteenth
century between the day-loving butterfly and the
night-flying moth, the only kind of "moughtes"
known to more remote generations being that
"sensible beaste," which "hydeth hym selfe
within the clothe that unneth he is seen," and
against whose ravages "they that sell woollen
Clothes use to wrap up the skin of a Bird called
the Kings-Fisher amongst them, or else hang one
in the shop, as a thing by a secret Antipathy that
Moths cannot endure."

The question as to whether butterflies are birds or
beasts repeats itself in the matter of the bee. Nor
would it be wise to venture a rash decision, seeing
that we have biblical authority for declaring that
it is both, with a slight flavour of the vegetable
kingdom, the writer of Ecclesiasticus asserting
that "the Bey is but a small beast among the
foules, yet is his frute exceedinge swete." Bartholomew is much of the same opinion, with a
leaning towards the animal theory, for he says
that "the bee is a lyttell shorte beaste with many
fete. And thoughe he myghte be acounted

amonge Volatiles, yet for he useth fete and goth
upon them, he may ryghtfully be accoumpted
amonge bestes that goo on grounde." Muffet, on
the other hand, is most contemptuous of such a
classification and declares that " He that writ the
Garden of Health seemed to dote much by con-
fidently affirming that Bees were fourfooted beasts,
for Nature only bestowed on them four feet, that
they might go upright and not more, lest it might
hinder their flying. But omitting this futile
Author, let us more amply describe this most
profitable and wise Insect."

It would be difficult to the verge of impossi-
bility to invent any legend more remarkable than
the true life-story of the bee, but with a proper
lack of observation and a genius for the misinter-
pretation of such things as are observed an
imaginative person can at least produce something
quite different from the facts. To begin with, it
is important to remember that there are three
types of bees, according as they are generated
from the carcasses of lions, bulls, or calves, and
the beekeeper will probably find it wiser, as well
as easier, to avoid the first class, as they are apt
to be bad-tempered. Whatever its origin, each
community is ruled by a king, who is chosen " by
due advice and circumspect choice," though the
monarchy is evidently to some extent hereditary,
as " the Royal race is not begotten a little worm
at the first as the Bees are, but presently able to
fly." Strict obedience to the ruler appears to be
enforced by the Eastern institution of hara-kiri,
for " Bees that are unobedient to the kyng, they
deme them selfe by their own dome for to dye by
the wounde of theyr owne stynge." Moreover,

the king, when occasion arises, does not hesitate
to display the stern impartiality of a Brutus, and
" if he chance to find amongst his young ones any
one that is a fool, unhandsome, hairy, of an angry
disposition or naturally ill-conditioned, by the
unanimous consent of the rest he gives order to
put him to death." One cannot help feeling how
different the history of the world would have been
and how much misery men might have been spared
had this salutary and eugenic custom prevailed
among human monarchs. Even in the ranks of
the commoners the wisdom of Solomon is found,
and the bees, patiently as they sit on their eggs
and careful as they are of their children, set them
to work when they are only three days old, so that
they shall not develop idle tendencies and imitate
the drones, which, like their human counterparts,
" are not famous either for manners or ingenuity."
Discipline, indeed, is the motto of the hive ; " in
the morning they are all still and silent till such
time as the Master-Bee gives three hums and
raiseth them up." Then off they go to their work
and all their various duties. " The more ancient
and graver sort of Bees are chosen to be the Kings
Lifeguard. Others of them administer Physick
and undertake to cure such as are sick ; and of
the Annise flowers, Saffron and Violet collect
together, compound and give them to drink a most
medicinable and cordial Honey." Besides these
dispensers and nurses there are the humbler
orderlies and attendants, of whom " some bear
water to the King and to such of the Bees that
are spent with old age and are discrepit." Oddly
enough, there is no mention of the kindly voluntary
workers who come round when they have a little

spare time to take the poor old bees out for a little airing in their Bath chairs; but it is a pretty picture. When the day's work is done they amuse themselves—possibly with music, but not apparently with dancing, as " they cannot dance by measure or according to the just number of paces, as the Elephant is said to do "—after all, the construction of the two beasts is somewhat dissimilar and it does not seem reasonable to reproach either for failing to rival the other; and an elephant trying to creep into a foxglove would probably be quite as absurd as a bee attempting to dance a fox-trot. Whatever amusements the bees have in the evening, it is enough for us that they enjoy themselves and " are noisy until the Captain of the Watch flies about and makes a buzzing, after which signal given, they are all so husht and still that if you lay your ear to the Hives mouth you cannot perceive the least noise."

Bees naturally suggest that ' poorest bugge that creeps," the laborious and moral ant, whose ways, despite Solomon's advice, I decline to consider, except in the light of an awful warning; for surely no other creature expends time and energy with such lavish prodigality to effect so little. My sympathies are entirely on the side of the cheerful and improvident grasshoppers, though I have never been so enthralled by their singing as to imitate the ancient Greeks in keeping them in cages. Most moralists, led astray by La Fontaine and Solomon, regard the frittering grass-hopper as the antithesis of the ant and therefore a reprobate and idle vagabond, one of Nature's strolling players, who is lucky to escape a whipping. Dr. Muffet with wider generosity commends it as superior to the clergy of his time: "The Grasshoppers hold on singing from morning to night, without intermission, very pleasant and sweetly; whereas many Preachers neither preach well nor often, scarce four times throughout the year; truly they may be ashamed, being bred more civilly, to be admonished of their duty by a wilde musician." He further points out that grasshoppers sing all one tune and are friends to one another and that they sing more loudly if you tickle their bellies; in all of which respects he asserts that they differ from preachers—though one has heard of a clergyman varying his grace to suit the lavishness of his host's table. In one other respect these insects are different from, but not necessarily superior to, mankind in general, for "amongst the Grasshoppers the females are silent—but our women have more tongue by far than men." Most remarkable of all the members of the tribe are the Silician "gressehoppers, havinge streyte veynes under the throte; whiche, havinge theire heddes kytte off, synge more swetely as hit is seyd, than when they have theire hedes, and dedde better than on lyve. Wherefore the schepardes, wyllinge to make them to synge swetely, kytte off their hedes." Probably this is another point in which they differ from human beings, but there are certain drawing-room amateurs, known to most of us, on whom it would at any rate be worth trying the experiment.

PRINTED BY
JARROLD AND SONS LTD.
NORWICH

METHUEN'S GENERAL LITERATURE

A SELECTION OF

Messrs. Methuen's

PUBLICATIONS

This Catalogue contains only a selection of the more important books published by Messrs. Methuen. A complete catalogue of their publications may be obtained on application.

ARMSTRONG (Warwick W.).
THE ART OF CRICKET. *Third Edition.* Illustrated. Crown 8vo, 3s. net.

BAIN (F. W.).
IN THE GREAT GOD'S HAIR. A DRAUGHT OF THE BLUE. AN INCARNATION OF THE SNOW. A MINE OF FAULTS. A DIGIT OF THE MOON. THE LIVERY OF EVE. A HEIFER OF THE DAWN. AN ESSENCE OF THE DUSK. THE DESCENT OF THE SUN. THE ASHES OF A GOD. BUBBLES OF THE FOAM. A SYRUP OF THE BEES. THE SUBSTANCE OF A DREAM. Fcap. 8vo, 5s. net each. AN ECHO OF THE SPHERES. Wide Demy 8vo, 10s. 6d. net.

BAKER (C. H. Collins).
CROME. Illustrated. Quarto, £5 5s. net.

BELLOC (H.).
A HISTORY OF ENGLAND. In 4 vols. Illustrated. Vols. I and II. Each, Demy 8vo, 15s. net. MARIE ANTOINETTE. Illustrated. Demy 8vo, 18s. net. PARIS. THE PYRENEES. Each, Illustrated, Crown 8vo, 8s. 6d. net. ON NOTHING. HILLS AND THE SEA. ON SOMETHING. FIRST AND LAST. THIS AND THAT AND THE OTHER. ON. Each, Fcap. 8vo, 3s. 6d. net. ON EVERYTHING. ON ANYTHING. Each, Fcap. 8vo, 6s. net.

BOWEN (Frank C.).
THE KING'S NAVY. Illustrated. Fcap. 4to, 7s. 6d. net.

BRAY (Sir Denys).
THE ORIGINAL ORDER OF SHAKESPEARE'S SONNETS. Crown 8vo, 5s. net.

BURTON (Robert).
BURTON THE ANATOMIST. Being extracts from Robert Burton's "Anatomy of Melancholy." Edited by G. C. F. Mead and R. C. Clift. Fcap. 8vo, 5s. net.

2

BUTLER (Kathleen T.).

A HISTORY OF FRENCH LITERATURE. Two Vols. Each Crown 8vo, 10s. 6d. net.

CAMPBELL (Olwen Ward).

SHELLEY AND THE UNROMANTICS. Illustrated. *Second Edition.* Demy 8vo, 16s. net.

CHANDLER (Arthur), D.D., late Lord Bishop of Bloemfontein.

ARA CŒLI. *Eighth Edition.* 5s. net. FAITH AND EXPERIENCE. *Third Edition.* 5s. net. THE CULT OF THE PASSING MOMENT. *Fifth Edition.* 6s. net. THE ENGLISH CHURCH AND RE-UNION. 5s. net. SCALA MUNDI. 4s. 6d. net.

CHESTERTON (G. K.).

ALARMS AND DISCURSIONS. A MISCELLANY OF MEN. THE USES OF DIVERSITY. THE OUTLINE OF SANITY. Each 6s. net. ALL THINGS CONSIDERED. TREMENDOUS TRIFLES. FANCIES VERSUS FADS. CHARLES DICKENS. THE BALLAD OF THE WHITE HORSE. Each 3s. 6d. net. WINE, WATER, AND SONG. 1s. 6d. net.

COLLISON-MORLEY (Lacy).

NAPLES THROUGH THE CENTURIES. Illustrated. Demy 8vo, 10s. 6d. net.

COWLING (George H.).

A PREFACE TO SHAKESPEARE. Illustrated. Crown 8vo, 5s. net.

DARK (Sidney) and GREY (Rowland).

W. S. GILBERT : HIS LIFE AND LETTERS. Illustrated. *Second Edition.* Demy 8vo, 15s. net.

DICKINSON (G. Lowes).

THE GREEK VIEW OF LIFE. *Fifteenth Edition.* Crown 8vo, 5s. net.

DOLLS' HOUSE (THE QUEEN'S).

THE BOOK OF THE QUEEN'S DOLLS' HOUSE. VOL. I. THE HOUSE. Edited by A. C. BENSON, C.V.O., and SIR LAWRENCE WEAVER, K.B.E. VOL. II. THE LIBRARY. Edited by E. V. LUCAS. Illustrated. Crown 4to, £6 6s. net. EVERYBODY'S BOOK OF THE QUEEN'S DOLLS' HOUSE. Illustrated. *Second Edition.* Crown 4to, 5s. net.

DREVER (James).

THE PSYCHOLOGY OF EVERYDAY LIFE. 6s. net. THE PSYCHOLOGY OF INDUSTRY. 5s. net.

EINSTEIN (Albert).

RELATIVITY : THE SPECIAL AND THE GENERAL THEORY. *Seventh Edition.* Crown 8vo, 5s. net. SIDELIGHTS ON RELATIVITY. Crown 8vo, 3s. 6d. net. THE MEANING OF RELATIVITY. Crown 8vo, 5s. net.

Other Books on the **Einstein Theory :**

THE PRINCIPLE OF RELATIVITY. By ALBERT EINSTEIN, H. A. LORENTZ, H. MINKOWSKI, and H. WEYL. With Notes by A. SOMMERFELD. Demy 8vo, 12s. 6d. net. EINSTEIN'S THEORY OF RELATIVITY. By MAX BORN. Demy 8vo, 12s. net. THE FOUNDATIONS OF EINSTEIN'S THEORY OF GRAVITATION. By ERWIN FREUNDLICH. Crown 8vo. 6s. net.

Write for Complete List

"EVOE" (E. V. KNOX).

PARODIES REGAINED. 5s. net. THESE LIBERTIES. 4s. 6d. net. FICTION AS SHE IS WROTE. FANCY NOW ! QUAINT SPECIMENS. Each 6s. net.

FITZGERALD (Edward).

THE RUBAIYAT OF OMAR KHAYYAM. Illustrated by EDMUND J. SULLIVAN. Wide Crown 8vo, 10s. 6d. net.

FYLEMAN (Rose).

FAIRIES AND CHIMNEYS. *Twentieth Edition.* THE FAIRY GREEN. *Tenth Edition.* THE FAIRY FLUTE. *Eighth Edition.* THE RAINBOW CAT AND OTHER STORIES. *Second Edition.* FORTY GOOD-NIGHT TALES. *Fifth Edition.* EIGHT LITTLE PLAYS FOR CHILDREN. *Third Edition.* FAIRIES AND FRIENDS. THE ADVENTURE CLUB. Each 3s. 6d. net. A SMALL CRUSE. Fcap. 8vo, 4s. 6d. net. THE ROSE FYLEMAN FAIRY BOOK. Crown 4to, 10s. 6d. net.

GIBBON (Edward).

THE DECLINE AND FALL OF THE ROMAN EMPIRE. Edited, with Notes, Appendices, and Maps, by J. B. BURY. Illustrated. Seven Volumes. Demy 8vo, each 12s. 6d. net. Also, unillustrated. Seven Volumes. Crown 8vo, each 7s. 6d. net.

GLOVER (T. R.).

THE CONFLICT OF RELIGIONS IN THE EARLY ROMAN EMPIRE. 10s. 6d. net. POETS AND PURITANS. 10s. 6d. net. VIRGIL. 10s. 6d. net. FROM PERICLES TO PHILIP. 10s. 6d. net.

GOTCH (J. A.).

OLD ENGLISH HOUSES. Illustrated. Demy 8vo, 16s. net.

GRAHAM (Harry).

THE WORLD WE LAUGH IN : MORE DEPORTMENTAL DITTIES. Illustrated by "FISH." *Sixth Edition.* Fcap. 8vo, 5s. net.

GRAHAME (Kenneth).

THE WIND IN THE WILLOWS. *Nineteenth Edition.* Crown 8vo, 7s. 6d. net. Also, illustrated by NANCY BARNHART. Small 4to, 10s. 6d. net.

HADFIELD (J. A.).

PSYCHOLOGY AND MORALS. *Sixth Edition.* Crown 8vo, 6s. net.

HALL (H. R.).

THE ANCIENT HISTORY OF THE NEAR EAST. Illustrated. *Sixth Edition, Revised.* Demy 8vo, £1 1s. net. THE CIVILIZATION OF GREECE IN THE BRONZE AGE. Illustrated. Demy 8vo. 10s. 6d. net.

HEWLETT (Maurice).

THE LETTERS OF MAURICE HEWLETT. Edited by LAURENCE BINYON. Illustrated. Demy 8vo, 18s. net.

HOLDSWORTH (W. S.).

A HISTORY OF ENGLISH LAW. Nine Volumes. Demy 8vo. Each £1 5s. net.

HUTTON (Edward).

THE CITIES OF SICILY. Illustrated. 10s. 6d. net. MILAN AND LOMBARDY. THE CITIES OF ROMAGNA AND THE MARCHES. SIENA AND SOUTHERN TUSCANY. VENICE AND VENETIA. THE CITIES OF SPAIN. NAPLES AND SOUTHERN ITALY. Each, illustrated, 8s. 6d. net. A WAYFARER IN UNKNOWN TUSCANY. THE CITIES OF UMBRIA. COUNTRY WALKS ABOUT FLORENCE. ROME. FLORENCE AND NORTHERN TUSCANY. Each, illustrated, 7s. 6d. net.

INGE (W. R.), C.V.O., D.D., Dean of St. Paul's.

CHRISTIAN MYSTICISM. (The Bampton Lectures of 1899.) *Sixth Edition.* Crown 8vo, 7s. 6d. net.

KIPLING (Rudyard).

BARRACK-ROOM BALLADS. 241st *Thousand*. THE SEVEN SEAS. 172nd *Thousand*. THE FIVE NATIONS. 138th *Thousand*. DEPARTMENTAL DITTIES. 111th *Thousand*. THE YEARS BETWEEN. 95th *Thousand*. Four editions of these famous volumes of poems are now published, viz. :—Crown 8vo, Buckram, 7s. 6d. net ; Fcap. 8vo, Cloth, 6s. net ; Leather, 7s. 6d. net ; and *Service Edition*. Two Vols. each book. Square Fcap. 8vo, 3s. 6d. net each Vol. A KIPLING ANTHOLOGY— VERSE. *Third Edition*. Cloth, 6s. net ; Leather, 7s. 6d. net. TWENTY POEMS. 423rd *Thousand*. 1s. net. A CHOICE OF SONGS. *Second Edition*. 2s. net.

LAMB (Charles and Mary).

THE COMPLETE WORKS. Edited by E. V. LUCAS. A New and Revised Edition in six volumes. With Frontispieces. Fcap. 8vo. Each 6s. net. The Volumes are :—1, MISCELLANEOUS PROSE. 2, ELIA AND THE LAST ESSAYS OF ELIA. 3, BOOKS FOR CHILDREN. 4, PLAYS AND POEMS. 5 and 6, LETTERS.
SELECTED LETTERS. Chosen and Edited by G. T. CLAPTON. Fcap. 8vo, 3s. 6d. net. THE CHARLES LAMB DAY BOOK. Compiled by E. V. LUCAS. Fcap. 8vo. 6s. net.

LANKESTER (Sir Ray).

SCIENCE FROM AN EASY CHAIR. First Series. SCIENCE FROM AN EASY CHAIR. Second Series. DIVERSIONS OF A NATURALIST. SECRETS OF EARTH AND SEA. (8s. 6d. net.) GREAT AND SMALL THINGS. Each illustrated. Crown 8vo, 7s. 6d. net.

LODGE (Sir Oliver).

MAN AND THE UNIVERSE, 7s. 6d. net. THE SURVIVAL OF MAN, 7s. 6d. net. REASON AND BELIEF, 2s. net. THE SUBSTANCE OF FAITH, 2s. net. RAYMOND, 10s. 6d. net. RAYMOND REVISED, 6s. net. RELATIVITY, 1s. net.

LUCAS (E. V.).

THE LIFE OF CHARLES LAMB. 2 Vols. £1 1s. net. EDWIN AUSTIN ABBEY, R.A. 2 Vols. £6 6s. net. VERMEER OF DELFT. 10s. 6d. net. A WANDERER IN ROME. A WANDERER IN HOLLAND. A WANDERER IN LONDON. LONDON REVISITED (REVISED). A WANDERER IN PARIS. A WANDERER IN FLORENCE. A WANDERER IN VENICE. Each 10s. 6d. net. A WANDERER AMONG PICTURES. 8s. 6d. net. E. V. LUCAS'S LONDON. 15s. net. THE OPEN ROAD. 6s. net. Also, illustrated by CLAUDE A. SHEPPERSON. 10s. 6d. net. Also, India Paper. Leather, 7s. 6d. net. THE FRIENDLY TOWN. FIRESIDE AND SUNSHINE. CHARACTER AND COMEDY. Each 6s. net. THE GENTLEST ART. 6s. 6d. net. THE SECOND POST. 6s. net. Also bound together, thin paper. 7s. 6d. net. HER INFINITE VARIETY. GOOD COMPANY. ONE DAY AND ANOTHER. OLD LAMPS FOR NEW. LOITERER'S HARVEST. CLOUD AND SILVER. A BOSWELL OF BAGHDAD. 'TWIXT EAGLE AND DOVE. THE PHANTOM JOURNAL. GIVING AND RECEIVING. LUCK OF THE YEAR. ENCOUNTERS AND DIVERSIONS. ZIGZAGS IN FRANCE. Each 6s. net. SPECIALLY SELECTED. URBANITIES. Each, illustrated by G. L. STAMPA, 7s. 6d. net. YOU KNOW WHAT PEOPLE ARE. Illustrated by GEORGE MORROW. 5s. net. PLAYTIME AND COMPANY. Illustrated by E. H. SHEPARD. 7s. 6d. net. THE SAME STAR : A Comedy in Three Acts. 3s. 6d. net. THE BRITISH SCHOOL.

6s. net. LITTLE BOOKS ON GREAT MASTERS. Each 5s. net. ROVING EAST AND ROVING WEST. 5s. net. See also DOLLS' HOUSE (THE QUEEN'S) and LAMB (CHARLES).

LYND (Robert).

THE BLUE LION. THE PEAL OF BELLS. Each, Fcap. 8vo, 3s. 6d. net. THE MONEY BOX. THE ORANGE TREE. Each, Fcap. 8vo. 6s. net.

McDOUGALL (William).

AN INTRODUCTION TO SOCIAL PSYCHOLOGY (*Twentieth Edition*), 10s. 6d. net ; BODY AND MIND (*Sixth Edition*), 12s. 6d. net ; AN OUTLINE OF PSYCHOLOGY, 12s. net ; NATIONAL WELFARE AND NATIONAL DECAY, 6s. net. ETHICS AND SOME MODERN WORLD PROBLEMS, 7s. 6d. net. AN OUTLINE OF ABNORMAL PSYCHOLOGY. 12s. 6d. net.

MAETERLINCK (Maurice).

THE BLUE BIRD, 6s. net and 2s. 6d. net. THE BETROTHAL, 6s. net, paper 3s. 6d. net. MARY MAGDALENE, 5s. net and 2s. net. DEATH, 3s. 6d. net. OUR ETERNITY, 6s. net. THE UNKNOWN GUEST, 6s. net. THE WRACK OF THE STORM, 6s. net. THE MIRACLE OF SAINT ANTHONY, 3s. 6d. net. THE BURGOMASTER OF STILEMONDE, 5s. net. MOUNTAIN PATHS 6s. net. TYLTYL, Told for Children (illustrated), 21s. net. (All Translated by A. TEIXEIRA DE MATTOS). POEMS, 5s. net (Done into English by BERNARD MIALL). THE CLOUD THAT LIFTED AND THE POWER OF THE DEAD (Translated by F. M. ATKINSON), 7s. 6d. net. THE GREAT SECRET (Translated by BERNARD MIALL), 7s. 6d. net.

METHUEN (Sir A.).

AN ANTHOLOGY OF MODERN VERSE. *107th Thousand.* SHAKESPEARE TO HARDY : An Anthology of English Lyrics. *15th Thousand.* Each, Fcap. 8vo, Cloth, 6s. net ; Leather, 7s. 6d. net.

MILNE (A. A.).

NOT THAT IT MATTERS. *Fifth Edition.* IF I MAY. *Fourth Edition.* Each 3s. 6d. net. WHEN WE WERE VERY YOUNG. *Twelfth Edition,* 102*nd Thousand.* Illustrated by E. H. SHEPARD. 7s. 6d. net. Leather 10s. 6d. net. FOR THE LUNCHEON INTERVAL. *Second Edition.* 1s. 6d. net.

MILNE (A. A.) and FRASER-SIMSON (H.).

FOURTEEN SONGS FROM "WHEN WE WERE VERY YOUNG." (*Sixth Edition.*) MORE SONGS (from the same). Each, Royal 4to. 7s. 6d. net. THE KING'S BREAKFAST. Music 8vo, 3s. 6d. net.

NEWMAN (Tom).

HOW TO PLAY BILLIARDS. Illustrated. Crown 8vo, 8s. 6d. net. BILLIARD DO'S AND DONT'S. F'cap. 8vo, 2s. 6d. net.

MORGAN (Sir Herbert).

CAREERS FOR BOYS AND GIRLS. Crown 8vo. 6s. net.

OMAN (Sir Charles).

A HISTORY OF THE ART OF WAR IN THE MIDDLE AGES, A.D. 378–1485. *Second Edition, Revised and Enlarged.* 2 Vols. Illustrated. Demy 8vo, £1 16s. net.

OXENHAM (John).

Eight Volumes of Poems. Small Pott 8vo, 1s. 3d. net each volume. BEES IN AMBER. (2s. net.) ALL'S WELL. THE KING'S HIGH WAY. THE VISION SPLENDID. THE FIERY CROSS. HEARTS COURAGEOUS. HIGH ALTARS. ALL CLEAR !

PETRIE (Sir Flinders).
A HISTORY OF EGYPT. Illustrated. Six Volumes. Crown 8vo. 1, FROM THE IST TO XVITH DYNASTY (12s. net). 2, THE XVIITH AND XVIIITH DYNASTIES (9s. net). 3, XIXTH TO XXXTH DYNASTIES (12s. net). 4, PTOLEMAIC EGYPT. EDWYN BEVAN. (10s. 6d. net). 5, EGYPT UNDER ROMAN RULE. J. G. MILNE. (12s. net). 6, EGYPT IN THE MIDDLE AGES. STANLEY LANE-POOLE. (10s. net).

RALEIGH (Sir Walter).
THE LETTERS OF SIR WALTER RALEIGH. Edited by LADY RALEIGH. 2 Vols. Illustrated. Demy 8vo, £1 10s. net.

STEVENSON (R. L.).
THE LETTERS OF ROBERT LOUIS STEVENSON TO HIS FAMILY AND FRIENDS. Selected and Edited by SIR SIDNEY COLVIN. Four Volumes. *Fifth Edition.* Fcap. 8vo, 6s. net each.

TILDEN (W. T.).
THE ART OF LAWN TENNIS. Illustrated. Crown 8vo, 6s. net. LAWN TENNIS FOR YOUNG PLAYERS. LAWN TENNIS FOR CLUB PLAYERS. LAWN TENNIS FOR MATCH PLAYERS. Each illustrated. Fcap. 8vo, 2s. 6d. net. SINGLES AND DOUBLES. Illustrated. Crown 8vo, 6s. net. THE COMMON SENSE OF LAWN TENNIS. Illustrated. Crown 8vo, 5s. net.

TILESTON (Mary W.).
DAILY STRENGTH FOR DAILY NEEDS. *Thirty-first Edition.* Medium 16mo, 3s. 6d. net. Also, India Paper, Leather, 6s. net.

UNDERHILL (Evelyn).
MYSTICISM. *Tenth Edition.* Demy 8vo, 15s. net. THE LIFE OF THE SPIRIT AND THE LIFE OF TO-DAY. *Sixth Edition.* Crown 8vo, 7s. 6d. net.

VARDON (Harry).
HOW TO PLAY GOLF. Illustrated. *Eighteenth Edition.* Crown 8vo, 5s. net.

WATERHOUSE (Elizabeth).
A LITTLE BOOK OF LIFE AND DEATH. *Twenty-second Edition.* Small Pott 8vo, 2s. 6d. net.

WATERS (Helena L.).
THE FRENCH AND ITALIAN RIVIERAS. FROM DOLOMITES TO STELVIO. Illustrated. Each 7s. 6d. net. LAGO DI GARDA AND NEIGHBOURHOOD. Illustrated. 6s. net.

WILDE (Oscar).
THE WORKS OF OSCAR WILDE. Sixteen Volumes. Fcap. 8vo, each 6s. 6d. net. Some also Fcap. 8vo, 2s. 6d. net. 1, LORD ARTHUR SAVILE'S CRIME AND THE PORTRAIT OF MR. W. H. 2, THE DUCHESS OF PADUA. 3, POEMS. 4, LADY WINDERMERE'S FAN. 5, A WOMAN OF NO IMPORTANCE. 6, AN IDEAL HUSBAND. 7, THE IMPORTANCE OF BEING EARNEST. 8, A HOUSE OF POMEGRANATES. 9, INTENTIONS. 10, DE PROFUNDIS AND PRISON LETTERS. 11, ESSAYS. 12, SALOME, A FLORENTINE TRAGEDY, AND LA SAINTE COURTISANE. 13, A CRITIC IN PALL MALL. 14, SELECTED PROSE OF OSCAR WILDE. 15, ART AND DECORATION. 16, FOR LOVE OF THE KING: A Burmese Masque (5s. net).

A SELECTION OF SERIES

THE ANTIQUARY'S BOOKS

Each, illustrated, Demy 8vo, 10s. 6d. net. A series of volumes dealing with various branches of English Antiquities, comprehensive and popular, as well as accurate and scholarly.

THE ARDEN SHAKESPEARE

Demy 8vo, 6s. net each volume.

An edition of Shakespeare in Single Plays. Edited with a full Introduction, Textual Notes, and a Commentary at the foot of the page. The edition is now complete in thirty-nine volumes.

CLASSICS OF ART

Edited by Dr. J. H. W. Laing.

Illustrated. Wide Royal 8vo, from 15s. net to £3 3s. net. A Library of Art dealing with Great Artists and with branches of Art.

THE "COMPLETE" SERIES

Illustrated. Demy 8vo, from 5s. net to 18s. net. A series of books on the chief Sports and Pastimes, comprehensive, lucid and authoritative.

THE CONNOISSEUR'S LIBRARY

Illustrated. Wide Royal 8vo, 31s. 6d. net.

European Enamels; Fine Books; Glass; Goldsmiths' and Silversmiths' Work; Ivories; Jewellery; Mezzotints; Porcelain; Seals.

EIGHT BOOKS BY R. S. SURTEES

With the Original Illustrations in Colour by J. Leech and others.

Fcap. 8vo, 6s. net and 7s. 6d. net.

Ask Mamma; Handley Cross; Hawbuck Grange; Hillingdon Hall; Jorrocks's Jaunts and Jollities; Mr. Sponge's Sporting Tour; Mr. Facey Romford's Hounds; Plain or Ringlets?

THE LITTLE GUIDES

Illustrated and with Maps. 60 Volumes. Small Pott 8vo, 4s. net mostly.

Pocketable Guides to the Counties of England and Wales and to well-known Districts at Home and Abroad.

MODERN MASTERPIECES

Fcap. 8vo, 3s. 6d. each volume.

Works by A. A. Milne, Joseph Conrad, Arnold Bennett, G. K. Chesterton, E. V. Lucas, H. Belloc, W. H. Hudson, R. L. Stevenson, Jack London, E. V. Knox and Robert Lynd.

PLAYS

Fcap. 8vo, 3s. 6d. net.

Kismet (Paper, 2s. net); Milestones; An Ideal Husband; The Ware Case; General Post; The Great Adventure; The Honeymoon; Across the Border (Crown 8vo); The Same Star.

METHUEN'S HALF-CROWN AND TWO SHILLING LIBRARIES

These are series of copyright books which have been such a popular success. They contain more books by distinguished writers than any other series.

Write for Complete Lists